VIRGIL
His Poetry through the Ages

VIRGIL

HIS POETRY THROUGH THE AGES

R. D. WILLIAMS

AND

T. S. PATTIE

The British Library

Cover illustrations
(Front) Virgil, detail from a third-century Roman mosaic now in the Bardo
National Museum Tunis; photograph by Roger Wood, London.
(Back) Virgil, classical bust in the Museo Capitolino, Rome; photograph
from the Mansell Collection.

Published by the British Library
Reference Division Publications
Great Russell Street
London WC1B 3DG

British Library Cataloguing in Publication Data

Williams, R.D.
  Virgil: his poetry through the ages.
  1. Virgil—Criticism and interpretation
  I. Title   II. Pattie, T.S.
  871'.01   PA6825
  ISBN 0 7123-0006-6
  ISBN 0-7123-0005-8 Pbk

Designed by John Mitchell
Phototypeset by Tradespools Ltd, Frome, Somerset
Printed in Great Britain by Biddles Ltd, Guildford, Surrey

Contents

Introduction: Virgil's Life and Times vii

PART I

VIRGIL AND HIS POETRY

1 *The Eclogues* 3
2 *The Georgics* 12
3 *The Aeneid* 21
4 *Virgil Today* 57

PART II

VIRGIL THROUGH THE AGES

5 *The Tradition of the Text* 73
6 *The Popular Traditions* 84
7 *Virgil's Imitators* 94
8 *Virgil in English* 109

Selective Bibliography 123
APPENDIX 1: Latin Manuscripts of Virgil in the British Library 125
APPENDIX 2: Latin Manuscripts of Virgil in the British Library:
Commentaries and Anthologies 139
APPENDIX 3: Manuscript Translations of Virgil in the British
Library 142

This book is published to accompany an exhibition *Virgil: the 2000th anniversary* held in the British Library exhibition galleries from September 1982 until February 1983. Permission from the Executors of the Estate of C. Day Lewis and from Jonathan Cape Ltd to use C. Day Lewis's translations of Virgil is gratefully acknowledged.

INTRODUCTION:
Virgil's Life and Times

Virgil (PUBLIUS VERGILIUS MARO) was born on 15
October 70 BC, near Mantua in northern Italy, of peasant stock.
His boyhood was spent on his father's farm, in the rich and
fertile valley of the River Po, and he was always essentially a
countryman at heart; he was shy in company, and did not enter
the world of business and politics, but in due course his poetry
brought him into close contact with many of the important
people of the Roman state, including Maecenas, the leading
patron of literature, and the Emperor Augustus himself. He
studied at Cremona, Milan, and finally Rome, immersing
himself in Greek literature and philosophy; he was influenced at
first by Epicureanism, but as time went on he turned rather
towards Stoicism. Soon he moved south to the area of Naples,
where he spent the rest of his life; the sixth book of the *Aeneid*
shows a fond familiarity with the Campanian countryside of
that part of Italy, and it was here that he was buried.

His earliest poetry, apart from one or two minor pieces of
doubtful authenticity, is a collection of pastoral poems called
the *Eclogues*, written probably between 42 and 37 BC. Next he
wrote the *Georgics* (37–30 BC) and finally the *Aeneid* (30–19 BC).
In 19 BC, intending to visit the Greek world to gain local colour
for the revision of the parts of the *Aeneid* set in that area, he fell
ill of a fever at the beginning of the voyage and died on his
return to Brundisium on 21 September of that year. His dying

instructions were that his poem should be burned (because it lacked the final revision) but the Emperor Augustus countermanded his request and ordered that the poem should be published with any necessary deletions but no additions. As we have it the *Aeneid* perhaps lacks some minor final touches, but it is not in any real sense an unfinished poem.

The period in which Virgil lived spanned the last years of the Roman Republic and the first few years of the Roman Empire under Augustus. By this time Rome had established her supremacy over the Mediterranean area, having long since defeated and destroyed her main rival, Carthage. Many of the lands bordering the Mediterranean had been made into Roman provinces, including Greece, by far the most highly civilized country of the ancient world. It was under Greek influence that the Romans had in the third century BC made their first faltering steps in the world of literature, art, philosophy, and science: in a famous epigram Horace wrote that 'conquered Greece took captive her fierce conqueror'. By Virgil's time Greek influence had pervaded the Roman world, and Roman literature, inspired by the Greeks, had produced the works of Ennius, Plautus, Terence, Catullus, Lucretius, Cicero. All of these authors, like Virgil himself, were greatly indebted to their Greek sources, but, again like Virgil, they used them as models on which to build something specially Roman.

The progress of Rome's achievements had at the time of Virgil's birth and for the first forty years of his life been marred and hampered by an unending series of grim civil wars. In 70 BC the memory of the civil war between the Roman generals Marius and Sulla in 88 to 86 BC was still fresh in people's minds, and it was followed by a period of great unrest and upheaval; the unscrupulous Catiline led a revolutionary movement which Cicero put down in 63 BC, and the developing rivalry between Pompey and Julius Caesar finally flared into full-scale civil war in 49 BC when Caesar with his army from Gaul crossed the

Introduction

Rubicon into Italy, drove Pompey's forces out of Italy and after defeating them in Greece, Spain, and Egypt established himself as the supreme ruler of the Roman world. This became more and more offensive to republican sentiment, and on the Ides of March in 44 BC Caesar was assassinated by the conspirators led by Brutus and Cassius. Mark Antony took up the cause of avenging Caesar's murder, and was joined by the young Octavian, later to become the Emperor Augustus. At Philippi in 42 BC the republican army led by Brutus and Cassius was defeated by Antony and Octavian. The way was open for the final confrontation between the two victors, and this ended at the sea-battle of Actium in 31 BC when Octavian won his final victory over Antony and his Egyptian ally Cleopatra, and became supreme in the Roman world.

Many Romans had for some time felt a deep sense of national guilt at the constant fighting between fellow country-men, and we find this guilt expressed in Horace's *Epodes* (e.g., 7 and 16) and in Virgil's *Eclogues* and *Georgics*. But along with sorrow for Rome's predicament, Virgil also expresses hope for the future, even before the battle of Actium, and increasingly so when it seemed more and more possible that Octavian would finally restore peace and prosperity to the war-weary world. And this is precisely what happened after the battle of Actium when the system of government known as the Roman Empire replaced the old republican regime. It was in this climate of relief and hope, indeed of optimism and rebirth, that the *Aeneid* was written. There were many, no doubt, who felt – as Cicero would have done had he still been alive – that the extinction of the republic marked a most undesirable loss of political freedom, but the new emperor was skilled at cloaking the autocratic aspects of his regime by at least seeming to retain traditional republican ways of life, and Virgil was emphatically among those who felt that Augustus was genuine in his policy of restoring old Roman traditions and building anew on the values of the past. Virgil's contemporary, Horace, had expressed these values with power and severity in his *Odes*, especially in the first six poems of Book 3, and they were also the values which emerge from the pages of the historian Livy, writing at the same time. Essentially they were values based on the simple virtues of the Romans of an older time, the virtues of bravery, steadfastness, loyalty, and above all of devotion to the gods and to one's family and country. The recurrent words are *fortitudo, pietas, religio, fides, disciplina.* These are the values which are reflected in the *Aeneid* – not unthinkingly, as we shall see, but with a conviction that in spite of their imperfections they offered ideals of conduct which would serve as a basis for national greatness and for the spread of world civilization.

R.D.W.

PART I

Virgil and his Poetry

R. D. WILLIAMS

I

THE ECLOGUES

T HE EARLIEST of Virgil's poems, apart from a few short
pieces most of which are of doubtful authenticity, are the ten
Eclogues ('Selections'), a series of pastoral poems based on the
Idylls of Theocritus, a Greek poet of *c*.270 BC. Those that are
closest to Theocritus present a world of shepherds in idyllic
country surroundings, singing to each other of their flocks or
their loves, often vying with each other in song contests. A
particularly fine example is the lament of Mopsus for the death
of Daphnis, the legendary prince of the shepherds, which is
balanced by Menalcas's song about how after his death Daphnis
became a god. Here is part of Mopsus's lament:

Exstinctum Nymphae crudeli funere Daphnin
flebant (vos coryli testes et flumina Nymphis),
cum complexa sui corpus miserabile nati,
atque deos atque astra vocat crudelia mater.
non ulli pastos illis egere diebus
frigida, Daphni, boves ad flumina; nulla neque amnem
libavit quadripes nec graminis attigit herbam.
Daphni, tuum Poenos etiam ingemuisse leones
interitum montesque feri silvaeque loquuntur.
Daphnis et Armenias curru subiungere tigris
instituit, Daphnis thiasos inducere Bacchi
et foliis lentas intexere mollibus hastas.

vitis ut arboribus decori est, ut vitibus uvae,
ut gregibus tauri, segetes ut pinguibus arvis,
tu decus omne tuis. postquam te fata tulerunt,
ipsa Pales agros atque ipse reliquit Apollo.   (5. 20–35)

Daphnis died. The nymphs bewailed his death –
    rivers and hazels heard them weeping:
'Cruel stars and gods!' his mother cried,
    clasping the poor corpse close in her arms.
No one drove his oxen to the stream,
    no beast ate or drank at all from sadness:
Even Afric lions roared their grief,
    forest and hill keened Daphnis dead.

Daphnis first enwreathed our wands with leaves,
    Daphnis was first to harness tigers,
Daphnis led the revellers through a dance –
    all for the Wine-god's festival day.
Vines grace elms, and grapes the vine,
    bulls grace herds and corn the joyous tillage:
Daphnis graced all nature – when he died,
    Corn-god and Song-god left us too.   (tr. Day Lewis)

And here is part of Menalcas's reply:

Candidus insuetum miratur limen Olympi
sub pedibusque videt nubes et sidera Daphnis.
ergo alacris silvas et cetera rura voluptas
Panaque pastoresque tenet Dryadasque puellas.
nec lupus insidias pecori, nec retia cervis
ulla dolum meditantur: amat bonus otia Daphnis.
ipsi laetitia voces ad sidera iactant
intonsi montes; ipsae iam carmina rupes,
ipsa sonant arbusta: 'deus, deus ille, Menalca!'   (5. 56–64)

4

The Eclogues

Daphnis shines at heaven's dazzling gate,
    under his feet sees clouds and planets.
Shepherds, nymphs and Pan are glad for this,
    forest and champaign quickened with joy.
Sheep nor deer have anything to dread –
    wolf or snare – for Daphnis loves the gentle:
Wooded hills, crags, orchards cry to heaven
    jocund hymns – 'A god is he!'

                                          (tr. Day Lewis)

But as well as his Theocritean pieces Virgil made certain important innovations in the pastoral genre which had a powerful influence on its subsequent development in European literature, culminating in poems like Milton's *Lycidas*. He did this in two main ways – one was to distance the rural settings of Theocritus into a semi-mythical Arcadia, a world further removed into an imaginary dream-land; and the other was to introduce into this idyllic never-never land contemporary political or social situations and sometimes real people, often important statesmen like Pollio or Gallus or Varus. Consequently some of these poems offer a tension between the potentially peaceful and delightful Arcadia, and the intrusion upon it and its ideals of military and political realities. We are confronted with a bewildering mixture of the artificial and the real, and many critics have been tempted to seek allegorical equivalents in real life for all of the shepherds in Arcadia. There is, however, no unanimity of identification (very far from it) and it seems better to keep the word allegory out of it, while at the same time allowing that some of the situations in the poems are based on Virgil's experiences in real life.

Outstanding examples of this are poems 1 and 9, both dealing with the expulsion of shepherds from their farms. While Virgil was writing these poems there were land confiscations on a large scale in order to settle the veteran soldiers of the

wars which raged after the death of Julius Caesar, and the story
goes that Virgil was one of those evicted, but that his farm was
later restored to him. At all events he portrays in these poems
the agony of the violation of the idyllic world of Arcadia by
harsh political realities. Here is a part of *Eclogue* I, spoken by
Meliboeus the exiled shepherd to his more fortunate friend
Tityrus who has been spared dispossession:

At nos hinc alii sitientis ibimus Afros,
pars Scythiam et rapidum cretae veniemus Oaxen
et penitus toto divisos orbe Britannos.
en umquam patrios longo post tempore finis,
pauperis et tuguri congestum caespite culmen,
post aliquot, mea regna, videns mirabor aristas?
impius haec tam culta novalia miles habebit,
barbarus has segetes. en quo discordia civis
produxit miseros: his nos consevimus agros!
insere nunc, Meliboee, piros, pone ordine vitis.
ite meae, felix quondam pecus, ite capellae.
non ego vos posthac viridi proiectus in antro
dumosa pendere procul de rupe videbo;
carmina nulla canam; non me pascente, capellae,
florentem cytisum et salices carpetis amaras.

(I. 64–78)

But the rest of us must go from here and be dispersed –
To Scythia, bone-dry Africa, the chalky spate of the Oxus,
Even to Britain – that place cut off at the very world's end.
Ah, when shall I see my native land again? after long years,
Or never? – see the turf-dressed roof of my simple cottage,
And wondering gaze at the ears of corn that were all my
    kingdom?
To think of some godless soldier owning my well-farmed fallow,
A foreigner reaping these crops! To such a pass has civil

The Eclogues

Dissension brought us: for people like these we have sown our fields.
Well, graft your pears, Meliboeus, and set your vines in rows.
Move onward, little she-goats, onward, once-happy flock!
No more shall I, stretched out in some green dingle here,
Watch you poised far off on the bushy brows of a hillside.
No more singing for me, no taking you to browse,
My little goats, on bitter willow and clover flower.

(tr. Day Lewis)

And here is a part of *Eclogue* 9, where the same fate has befallen Moeris, who tells his friend Lycidas of his sorrows:

Moeris: *O Lycida, vivi pervenimus, advena nostri*
              (quod numquam veriti sumus) ut possessor agelli
              diceret: 'haec mea sunt; veteres migrate coloni.'
              nunc victi, tristes, quoniam fors omnia versat,
              hos illi (quod nec vertat bene) mittimus haedos.

Lycidas: *Certe equidem audieram, qua se subducere colles*
              incipiunt mollique iugum demittere clivo,
              usque ad aquam et veteres, iam fracta cacumina, fagos,
              omnia carminibus vestrum servasse Menalcan.

Moeris: *Audieras, et fama fuit; sed carmina tantum*
              nostra valent, Lycida, tela inter Martia quantum
              Chaonias dicunt aquila veniente columbas.

(9. 2–13)

Moeris: Oh, Lycidas, that I should have lived to see an outsider
         Take over my little farm – a thing I had never feared –
         And tell me, 'You're dispossessed, you old tenants,
            you've got to go.'
         We're down and out. And look how Chance turns the
            tables on us –
         These are *his* goats (rot them!) you see me taking to.
            market.

Virgil and his Poetry

Lycidas: Can this be true? I had heard that all the land, from the
     place where
     That spur with its gentle slope juts out from the recessive
     Hill-line, as far as the water and the old beech-trees with
     Their shattered tops – all this had been saved by Menalcas' poetry.
Moeris: So you heard. That rumour did get about. But poems
     Stand no more chance, where the claims of soldiers are involved,
     Than do the prophetic doves if an eagle swoops upon them.

(tr. Day Lewis)

The sixth *Eclogue* is based on the poetry of Gallus, a prominent man of letters and politics of the time, and the tenth, an astonishing poem, tells in pastoral convention of Gallus's unhappy love for Lycoris. Near its beginning is a passage lamenting Gallus's fate which was closely imitated by Milton:

> *Quae nemora aut qui vos saltus habuere, puellae*
> *Naides, indigno cum Gallus amore peribat?*
> *nam neque Parnasi vobis iuga, nam neque Pindi*
> *ulla moram fecere, neque Aonie Aganippe.*
> *illum etiam lauri, etiam flevere myricae,*
> *pinifer illum etiam sola sub rupe iacentem*
> *Maenalus, et gelidi fleverunt saxa Lycaei.*
> *stant et oves circum; nostri nec paenitet illas,*
> *nec te paeniteat pecoris, divine poeta;*
> *et formosus ovis ad flumina pavit Adonis.*

(10. 9–18)

Young Naiads, oh where were you, haunting what
     woodland glades
Or groves, that time my Gallus was sick with hopeless love?
No duties kept you upon the ridges of Mount Parnassus
Or Pindus, or by the sacred spring at Helicon's foot.
Even the laurels, even the tamarisks wept for him

8

The Eclogues

Where under a crag he lay, alone: even pine-clad Maenalus
Wept in pity for him, and the cold cliffs of Lycaeus.
    The sheep were standing round you – they see no
        shame in our sorrows,
So think no shame of them, my heaven-sent poet: even
Exquisite Adonis grazed sheep beside a stream.

(tr. Day Lewis)

This is the passage from Milton's *Lycidas*:

Where were ye Nymphs when the remorseless deep
Closed o'er the head of your loved Lycidas?
For neither were ye playing on the steep
Where your old Bards, the famous Druids lie,
Nor on the shaggy top of Mona high,
Nor yet where Deva spreads her wizard stream . . .

(50–55)

By far the most famous of the *Eclogues* is the fourth poem, a prophecy of the birth of a child who will inaugurate a new Golden Age. This poem (written in 40 BC) is often called the Messianic Eclogue, and was regarded by many Christians as a prophecy of Christ. Virgil was thought of as a prophet, like Isaiah, who had foretold the birth of the Saviour, and this (along with the proto-Christian values of the *Aeneid*) contributed very largely to Virgil's enormous popularity in the Middle Ages, illustrated by the fact that Dante calls him his master, and chooses him as his guide to the very gates of Paradise. The poem is elevated and indeed hymnic in tone; it begins with a statement of its exceptional importance:

Sicelides Musae, paulo maiora canamus!
non omnis arbusta iuvant humilesque myricae;
si canimus silvas, silvae sint consule dignae.   (4. 1–3)

Virgil and his Poetry

Sicilian Muse, I would try now a somewhat grander theme.
Shrubberies or meek tamarisks are not for all; but if it's
Forests I sing, may the forests be worthy of a consul.

(tr. Day Lewis)

It continues with idyllic descriptions, sometimes reminiscent of Isaiah, of the happy age which the child's birth will inaugurate; here is part of it:

Teque adeo decus hoc aevi, te consule, inibit,
Pollio, et incipient magni procedere menses;
te duce, si qua manent sceleris vestigia nostri,
inrita perpetua solvent formidine terras.
ille deum vitam accipiet divisque videbit
permixtos heroas et ipse videbitur illis,
pacatumque reget patriis virtutibus orbem.
    At tibi prima, puer, nullo munuscula cultu
errantis hederas passim cum baccare tellus
mixtaque ridenti colocasia fundet acantho.
ipsae lacte domum referent distenta capellae
ubera, nec magnos metuent armenta leones;
ipsa tibi blandos fundent cunabula flores.
occidet et serpens, et fallax herba veneni
occidet; Assyrium vulgo nascetur amomum.
at simul heroum laudes et facta parentis
iam legere et quae sit poteris cognoscere virtus,
molli paulatim flavescet campus arista,
incultisque rubens pendebit sentibus uva,
et durae quercus sudabunt roscida mella.

(4. 11–30)

And it's while you are consul – you, Pollio – that this glorious
Age shall dawn, the march of its great months begin.
You at our head, mankind shall be freed from its age-long fear,
All stains of our past wickedness being cleansed away.

The Eclogues

This child shall enter into the life of the gods, behold them
Walking with antique heroes, and himself be seen of them,
And rule a world made peaceful by his father's virtuous acts.
    Child, your first birthday presents will come from
        nature's wild –
Small presents: earth will shower you with romping ivy, foxgloves,
Bouquets of gipsy lilies and sweetly-smiling acanthus.
Goats shall walk home, their udders taut with milk, and nobody
Herding them: the ox will have no fear of the lion:
Silk-soft blossom will grow from your very cradle to lap you.
But snakes will die, and so will fair-seeming, poisonous plants.
Everywhere the commons will breathe of spice and incense.
    But when you are old enough to read about famous men
And your father's deeds, to comprehend what manhood means,
Then a slow flush of tender gold shall mantle the great plains,
Then shall grapes hang wild and reddening on thorn-trees,
And honey sweat like dew from the hard bark of oaks.

(tr. Day Lewis)

Alexander Pope called the *Eclogues* 'the sweetest poems in the world'; it is a well-chosen adjective, for in a pastoral setting Virgil creates in limpid and sweet-sounding verse the idyllic world of an imaginary Arcadia. This is poetry mostly of a fairy and fragile world where suffering and pathos is muted and transformed into a gentle mood; its style is mannered and set in a minor key; it leads up to, but at the same time contrasts markedly with, the power and intensity which Virgil was to develop in the *Georgics* and the *Aeneid*.

2

THE GEORGICS

'THE BEST POEM of the best poet' was Dryden's verdict of the *Georgics*. This poem on farming, in four books of hexameters, was written over a period of seven years (37–30 BC), which works out at about a line a day: 'he licked his verses into shape as a she-bear her cubs', says the author of an ancient life. The *Georgics* stands with Horace's *Odes* as the most perfectly finished verse in Latin and indeed world literature.

The ostensible aim of the poem was to give instruction to farmers, and it is classed therefore as didactic poetry, but the instruction is not organized as in a technical textbook, nor does Virgil talk of the land in a farmer's terms, but in a highly poetical and sublimated rhetoric. The real intention was by means of poetic skill in description to inspire readers with a greater and deeper love for the Italian countryside and its plantations and farms. Virgil himself was a countryman who knew and loved rural Italy, and he harnessed all his uncanny skill in metre and diction to express this sincere passion for nature and its creatures and plants and trees. There is a warm pantheistic glow through the poem (not unlike Wordsworth's feeling for nature), and an insistence that all of nature is part, as man himself is part, of the total cosmos ordained by divine gift. Animals and plants will serve man if man treats them properly; the abundance of nature will be available to those who by their hard work merit it. Yet this optimism is qualified by intense

and vivid descriptions of times of disaster, not only failures
caused by man's neglect, but also events beyond his control,
such as forest fires, devastation of crops by storm and flood,
and of flocks by diseases and plague.

The first book tells of how to work the land – of
ploughing, drainage, and sowing, especially of corn; the second
book is about growing trees, especially the vine; the third is
about horses, cattle, and sheep; and the fourth is about bee-
keeping, ending with a mythological story about Aristaeus,
and the loss and restoration of his bees, which includes an inset
telling the story of how Orpheus lost Eurydice. Here at the end
of the *Georgics* we see the narrative skill and imaginative power
which were to characterize the *Aeneid*. The story is well-
known, and has inspired many dramatic and musical versions:
Eurydice had died of a snakebite while trying to escape from
Aristaeus's advances, and Orpheus was permitted to visit the
underworld to bring her back on condition that he did not look
round at her as she followed him out.

Iamque pedem referens casus evaserat omnis,
redditaque Eurydice superas veniebat ad auras
pone sequens (namque hanc dederat Proserpina legem),
cum subita incautum dementia cepit amantem,
ignoscenda quidem, scirent si ignoscere Manes:
restitit, Eurydicenque suam iam luce sub ipsa
immemor heu! victusque animi respexit. ibi omnis
effusus labor atque immitis rupta tyranni
foedera, terque fragor stagnis auditus Avernis.
illa 'quis et me' inquit 'miseram et te perdidit, Orpheu,
quis tantus furor? en iterum crudelia retro
fata vocant, conditque natantia lumina somnus.
iamque vale: feror ingenti circumdata nocte
invalidasque tibi tendens, heu non tua, palmas.'
dixit et ex oculis subito, ceu fumus in auras

Virgil and his Poetry

commixtus tenuis, fugit diversa, neque illum
prensantem nequiquam umbras et multa volentem
dicere praeterea vidit; nec portitor Orci
amplius obiectam passus transire paludem.   (4. 485–503)

And now he's avoided every pitfall of the homeward path,
And Eurydice, regained, is nearing the upper air
Close behind him (for this condition has Proserpine made),
When a moment's madness catches her lover off his guard –
Pardonable, you'd say, but Death can never pardon.
He halts. Eurydice, his own, is now on the lip of
Daylight. Alas! he forgot. His purpose broke. He looked back.
His labour was lost, the pact he had made with the
    merciless king
Annulled. Three times did thunder peal over the pools of
    Avernus.
'Who,' she cried, 'has doomed me to misery, who has
    doomed us?
What madness beyond measure? Once more a cruel fate
Drags me away, and my swimming eyes are drowned in
    darkness.
Good-bye. I am borne away. A limitless night is about me
And over the strengthless hands I stretch to you, yours no longer.'
Thus she spoke: and at once from his sight, like a wisp of smoke
Thinned into air, was gone.
Wildly he grasped at shadows, wanting to say much more,
But she did not see him; nor would the ferryman of the Inferno
Let him again cross the fen that lay between them.

                                              (tr. Day Lewis)

Each book of the *Georgics* begins with a dedication to
Maecenas, the right-hand man of the future Emperor Augustus, particularly renowned as a patron of letters, and there are
proud references to Augustus's achievements at the beginning

14

and end of Book 1, the beginning of Book 3, and the end of Book 4. But the poem should not be thought of as a commissioned work; certainly it chimed in well with the political needs of the time, to get the Romans back to the land that had been so neglected during the long series of civil wars, but it springs essentially and personally from Virgil's own intense love for the beauty of nature, his desire to express these feelings in verse, and his sorrow at the ravages inflicted on the countryside by civil war:

> *quippe ubi fas versum atque nefas; tot bella per orbem,*
> *tam multae scelerum facies, non ullus aratro*
> *dignus honos, squalent abductis arva colonis,*
> *et curvae rigidum falces conflantur in ensem.*   (1. 505–508)

> For Right and Wrong are confused here, there's so much
>   war in the world,
> Evil has so many faces, the plough so little
> Honour, the labourers are taken, the fields untended,
> And the curving sickle is beaten into the sword that yields not.
>   (tr. Day Lewis)

Instances of Virgil's passion for his subject are to be found throughout the poem, frequently obliquely, in his warm sensitivity, and sometimes directly, as in *Georgics* 3. 284ff.:

> *Sed fugit interea, fugit inreparabile tempus,*
> *singula dum capti circumvectamur amore . . .*
> *nec sum animi dubius verbis ea vincere magnum*
> *quam sit et angustis hunc addere rebus honorem;*
> *sed me Parnasi deserta per ardua dulcis*
> *raptat amor; iuvat ire iugis, qua nulla priorum*
> *Castaliam molli devertitur orbita clivo.*

>   (3.284–285, 289–293)

15

But in the meanwhile time is flying, flying beyond hope of recall while I recount all these things, captured by my love of them. . . . And I am not unaware how difficult it is to express it all in words, and to pay this tribute to humble themes [i.e., here sheep and goats]; but a sweet love whirls me on over the heights of Parnassus; it is my delight to tread high places where no path of any predecessor leads with its gentle slope to Castalia [the spring of the Muses on Mount Parnassus].

Or again in *Georgics* 2. 490–494:

Felix qui potuit rerum cognoscere causas,
atque metus omnis et inexorabile fatum
subiecit pedibus strepitumque Acherontis avari.
fortunatus et ille deos qui novit agrestis
Panaque Silvanumque senem Nymphasque sorores.

Happy the man who could understand the causes of things, and trample beneath his feet all fear and inexorable fate and the roar of greedy Acheron [a reference to Lucretius, Virgil's predecessor in didactic verse, whose philosophical poem expounded the doctrine of Epicureanism]. Fortunate also he [i.e., Virgil himself] who knows the gods of the countryside, Pan and old Silvanus and the sister Nymphs.

Here the final phrases indicate very clearly Virgil's attitude to the countryside as essentially a religious one: he sees the rural scene not only as a perfectly ordered part of the total divine creation, but also as actually populated by countless local divinities – Pan, Silvanus, Faunus, Nymphs, Dryads.

There are many other passages which intensely portray the joy of the farmer's life:

The Georgics

O fortunatos nimium, sua si bona norint,
agricolas! quibus ipsa procul discordibus armis
fundit humo facilem victum iustissima tellus. . . .
at secura quies et nescia fallere vita,
dives opum variarum, at latis otia fundis,
(speluncae vivique lacus et frigida Tempe
mugitusque boum mollesque sub arbore somni)
non absunt; illic saltus ac lustra ferarum,
et patiens operum exiguoque adsueta iuventus,
sacra deum sanctique patres; extrema per illos
Iustitia excedens terris vestigia fecit.

(2. 458–460, 467–474)

Happy are farmers, happy indeed if only they knew their
blessings: far from the clash of warfare the earth itself,
always a fair mistress, pours forth from the soil an easy
livelihood: (if they lack the specious luxuries of city life)
yet they have an unanxious mind, a life that cannot let
them down, rich in all sorts of wealth, peace in their wide
domains, grottoes, living lakes, cool valleys, the lowing of
cattle, gentle sleep beneath the trees, ... it was among
these farmers that the goddess Justice last stepped before
she departed from among us.

Another is the famous 'praises of Italy' passage (*Georgics* 2. 136–
176):

Hic ver adsiduum atque alienis mensibus aestas:
bis gravidae pecudes, bis pomis utilis arbos.
at rabidae tigres absunt et saeva leonum
semina, nec miseros fallunt aconita legentis,
nec rapit immensos orbis per humum neque tanto
squameus in spiram tractu se colligit anguis.
adde tot egregias urbes operumque laborem,

Virgil and his Poetry

tot congesta manu praeruptis oppida saxis
fluminaque antiquos subter labentia muros.

(2. 149–157)

Here spring is everlasting, and the summer extends into months not its own: the cattle bring forth their young twice a year, the apple tree produces fruit twice. There are no ravening tigers or fierce brood of lions, no deadly nightshade deceives the unwary pickers, no scaly snakes writhe in immense spirals or coil in mighty sweeps over the ground. Think too of our many lovely cities, the toil of men's efforts, all those towns we have built heaped high on their sheer cliffs and the rivers gliding beneath their ancient walls.

One of the outstanding methods by which Virgil achieves vividness in his more technical passages is to personify nature and its creatures and plants: the corn crop will 'respond to' the farmer's hopes if properly ploughed, and it is 'joyful' if cultivated properly; the apple-tree if not pruned correctly will 'forget its old flavours'; the tree properly grafted 'marvels at its new foliage and fruit not its own'. When you make your threshing-floor you must beware of pests or the mouse will 'set up house' underneath it, or the ant will carry off your grain 'anxiously providing against a poverty-stricken old age'. Bees especially are personified; they live under fixed laws, they set up their sentries, they have 'great hearts in their little bodies', they go forth to battle for their kings (Virgil, like all other Romans, thought the 'queens' were 'kings'), and above all they have a share in the divine spirit which permeates all living things (4. 219ff.). The animals closer to man are portrayed with particular sympathy: the young and spirited horse being trained for racing or battle (3. 179ff.), the sheep pathetically affected with disease which man must try to combat (3. 440ff.), the faithful oxen who go on pulling the plough even when stricken with mortal illness (3. 515ff.).

One of the most striking features of the *Georgics* is that it gives the first detailed presentation in antiquity of what we may call the dignity of labour. The perpetual theme of the poem is the need for hard work and how it is rewarded by the justice of nature: 'toil conquers all' (1. 145); 'indeed every farmer must devote himself to hard work' (2. 61); 'you must make all your preparations in advance if the glory of the divine countryside is to await you in its full measure' (1. 168)'; 'you must not relax your efforts, or you will be like a man in a boat rowing upstream who takes a rest and is swept headlong backwards' (1. 200ff.). This idea is expressed most fully in the mythology of the abolition of the Golden Age by Jupiter because he considered it was for man's benefit to earn his bread in the sweat of his brow:

> pater ipse colendi
> haud facilem esse viam voluit, primusque per artem
> movit agros, curis acuens mortalia corda
> nec torpere gravi passus sua regna veterno.
>
> (1. 121–124)

Jupiter himself did not wish the way of cultivation to be easy, and he first caused the fields to be ploughed, sharpening men's minds by anxieties, and he did not let his realm be slack and lazy.

Before Jupiter, men lived in a golden age with the earth providing everything without effort on their part, but Jupiter changed all that in order that experience and thought might forge the various skills, seek the corn-crop in the furrow, and make fire from flint, build boats, learn navigation by the stars, hunt, fish, saw wood, and learn many other skills. 'Toil won all the victories, relentless toil and need which drives us onwards in adversity' (1. 145–146).

The *Georgics* is above all a religious poem, exploring the situation and duties of man in a divinely ordained world. Nature with its animals and plants is divinely created and maintained, and man must play his proper part as the highest of nature's creations. This part essentially involves his acceptance of his natural environment and of his obligation to work hard at the tasks which are ever present. The rewards are rich, and the farmer should become a crucial part of 'the glory of the divine countryside'.

3

THE AENEID

ALL THROUGH HIS LIFE Virgil (like Milton) was planning
to crown his poetic achievements by writing a full-scale epic
poem, and we know that he considered and discarded various
possible subjects before finally choosing the legend of Aeneas,
the Trojan prince who under divine guidance voyaged from
burning Troy to found a new city in a western land which was
destined to become queen of the world. The date of the events
recounted in the *Aeneid* was early in the twelfth century BC,
nearly 1200 years before Virgil's own time. What advantages
did he gain from choosing such a subject, set in the very remote
past?

First and foremost he gained a freedom to shape his
material to his own wishes, as he could not have done with a
Roman theme nearer in time, where historical fact would have
limited poetic treatment. The story of Aeneas, though well-
known in Virgil's time, was very fluid, rather like our King
Arthur legend. This enabled the poet to recast and alter to suit
his poetic purposes; in particular he gave far greater emphasis to
the part of the story which told of Dido than had been the case
before. A second great advantage was that the events of which
he told were contemporary with the Homeric poems, the *Iliad*
and the *Odyssey*, which had cast their spell upon him. Thus he
could use these poems as a point of reference, recalling them,
reshaping them for his own purposes, and in particular

presenting Aeneas as a Homeric hero who steps out of the heroic world into a new world which has to formulate new ideals and aspirations appropriate for the future Romans. A third advantage was that with so antique a theme Virgil could without difficulty introduce Homer's Olympian deities into his poem, and indulge his delight in depicting scenes of fancy and imagination to vary the more realistic passages of man's activity in the actual world.

While he gained these advantages from having a theme set in the distant past, Virgil also avoided the danger of choosing a subject which might be insufficiently relevant to his deep desire to sing of the glories of his own country. His was a Roman theme, however far remote in time, and Aeneas is in a very real sense the first Roman. At the beginning of the third book of the *Georgics* Virgil had spoken of how he did not wish to sing of remote mythological themes but would rather tell of the glories of the new Roman empire; in the *Aeneid* his theme gave him the advantages of both types of narrative poetry.

Essentially, then, the poem operates on two time-scales: it is Homeric in its dramatic date and can therefore employ Homeric devices without a feeling of unreality, yet it is Augustan in its presentation of Roman values and achievements and aspirations. The linking of the distant past with the present is achieved by a number of methods: prophecy of the future (e.g., by Jupiter in Book 1); the vision of ghosts waiting to be born, at the end of Book 6; the pictures of future Roman history on the shield made for Aeneas, at the end of Book 8; and frequent aetiological allusions, where the origin or the cause of well-known Augustan features is referred to in the poem. Examples of this are the promise by Aeneas in Book 6 of a marble temple for Apollo, housing the Sibylline books – the collection of oracles consulted for political and legal guidance (Augustus had just built such a temple); the first performance of the Game of Troy in Book 5 (a feature of contemporary Roman life); the sacrifice to Hercules by Evander in Book 8 (the origin of the sacrifices held yearly in Virgil's time); and frequent name associations (like Julian – the name of the patrician family from which Augustus claimed descent as the adopted son of Julius Caesar – derived from Aeneas's son Iulus; Cape Palinurus called after Aeneas's lost helmsman, and so on).

The *Aeneid* is thus about how Roman values developed and superseded those of the heroic Homeric world, and more important still it is about timeless and universal problems of human behaviour – problems like the conflict between personal wishes and the compulsions of duty, the loyalties owed to gods, to family, to country, to friends. These are some of the human dilemmas which Virgil explores throughout the poem in countless poetically invented situations.

Virgil and his Poetry

The poem begins with Aeneas and his Trojan followers almost in sight of their goal in Italy after seven long years of wandering to try to find their promised land. They are off the coast of Sicily sailing north, but Juno – queen of the gods, arch-enemy of the Trojans – arouses a violent storm which drives them off course to the coast of Carthage. The hostility of Juno is ever-present in the poem, and Virgil gives various mythological reasons for this (the judgement of Paris, her jealousy of the Trojan youth Ganymede) and a historical one: she was the patron goddess of Carthage, Rome's greatest enemy in the Mediterranean world. But in a large sense she symbolizes the apparently senseless and unjustifiable suffering and disaster which strike mortal men, the power of Fortuna, the 'slings and arrows of outrageous Fortune'. Juno thus takes pride of place in Virgil's earliest presentation of his main theme. 'Can there be such anger in heavenly minds?' (I. 11) he asks at the close of his invocation to the Muse, an invocation which had asked not, as in Homer, to be inspired to recount the subject matter of his poem, but to give the causes of the events – *Musa, mihi causas memora.*

Within the first few hundred lines Virgil introduces us to many of his other major themes: we see him delighting in the imaginative description of a mythological scene as he tells of Aeolus controlling the winds shut up in his mountain, and their release to arouse a storm. He switches his descriptive method to a naturalistic account of great waves and whirlpools and sandbanks, and then back to mythology as Neptune calms the storm and rides over the serene waves in his chariot, accompanied by his retinue of sea-deities.

During the storm another major theme is introduced – the character of the hero. We meet Aeneas here for the first time in the poem, beset by a terrifying storm. How does he react?

The Aeneid

Calmly, with heartening speech to his men? No, he is terrified and wishes he had died at Troy. We are invited at the very beginning to see in Aeneas a man by no means possessed of superhuman resolution and courage, but rather a frail human whose strength may well prove to be unequal to his task. He and his followers survive the storm and are driven to the shores of Africa, where Aeneas manages to produce some heartening words; but Virgil tells us immediately that his confidence was only a pretence and that he was deeply anxious underneath (1. 208–209).

Now the scene switches to Olympus, where Aeneas's mother Venus complains bitterly to Jupiter that he had promised that her son after escaping from burning Troy was required by fate to found a great empire. Here he is, attempting to do what he is required to do, and he has had nothing but disaster encompassing him for seven long years. 'Is this the reward for devotion to duty?', she asks; *hic pietatis honos?* (1. 253). This word *pietas* is the special quality of Aeneas (one that the Romans learned from him) and his most frequent epithet in the poem is *pius*, 'devoted to duty'. Venus here echoes Virgil's own statement in the introduction to his poem: how can we understand why a man who is doing his best to fulfil a divine obligation nevertheless suffers greatly himself and causes great sufferings to others? This question is never answered, but it is explored in countless brilliantly devised situations.

Jupiter replies in a speech of serene optimism, one of the great expressions of patriotism in the poem. It is ironical that we the readers learn of the great future destined to come to Aeneas's descendants, but Aeneas himself, who does not, of course, hear the conversation of the gods, must continue to grope onwards without the inspiration of Jupiter's stirring phrases. 'To these Romans', says Jupiter, 'I set no bounds in space or time; I have given them rule without end.'

Virgil and his Poetry

His ego nec metas rerum nec tempora pono:
Imperium sine fine dedi.

(1. 278–279)

His speech ends with a reference to the destined rule of
Augustus over the wide world when the harsh generations will
become gentle and wars be laid aside, and the godless spirit of
Discord will be for ever chained and helpless, no longer able to
dominate human hearts as had been the case in so much of
Rome's history up to Virgil's time.

Aspera tum positis mitescent saecula bellis:
cana Fides et Vesta, Remo cum fratre Quirinus
iura dabunt; dirae ferro et compagibus artis
claudentur Belli portae; Furor impius intus
saeva sedens super arma et centum vinctus aënis
post tergum nodis fremet horridus ore cruento.

(1. 291–296)

Then dire debate and impious war shall cease,
And the stern age be softened into peace:
Then banished faith shall once again return,
And Vestal fires in hallowed temples burn,
And Remus with Quirinus shall sustain
The righteous laws, and fraud and force restrain.
Janus himself before his fane shall wait,
And keep the dreadful issues of his gate,
With bolts and iron bars; within remains
Imprisoned Fury, bound in brazen chains;
High on a trophy raised, of useless arms,
He sits, and threats the world with vain alarms.

(tr. Dryden)

The Aeneid

Now begins the story of Dido which is to dominate the first third of the poem, and which has proved over the centuries to be by far the most popular and widely read part of the whole poem. On his landing on the shores of Africa Aeneas is met by his goddess mother in disguise who tells him where he is and relates the story of how Dido has built a flourishing city in Carthage after having been driven from her home city of Tyre by the villainy of her brother. A vivid picture is built up of Dido's admirable qualities: she led her people away from disaster to a new world (the task which Aeneas has and which he is so far from fulfilling), and when she appears to Aeneas he meets a beloved and highly capable ruler, as beautiful as Diana, and kind and sympathetic towards those in need. She offers the Trojans generous help and hospitality, and tells them, 'Myself not unaware of suffering, I am learning to help those in distress'; *Non ignara mali miseris succurrere disco* (1. 630). It seems inconceivable that her life should fall in ruins about her, as it is destined to. The goddesses Juno and Venus scheme to make her fall helplessly in love with Aeneas, and undertones of impending tragedy colour the narrative as she holds a great feast for the Trojans and asks Aeneas to tell the story of his adventures.

Virgil and his Poetry

BOOK 2

This book and the next form a flashback in the narrative as Aeneas tells his story to Dido. Book 2 is about the events of a single fateful night, the night when Troy was destroyed. It is a book of intense and sustained tragedy, culminating in the murder at the altar of old King Priam by Achilles's son Pyrrhus. It begins with one of the most famous stories of antiquity, the device of the wooden horse and the entry of the Greeks into Troy concealed in its belly. Virgil tells this in a vivid and exciting fashion with the persuasive rhetoric of Sinon winning over the too credulous Trojans and the death of Laocoon who had opposed the entry of the horse. Here is the climax:

> *Dividimus muros et moenia pandimus urbis.*
> *accingunt omnes operi pedibusque rotarum*
> *subiciunt lapsus, et stuppea vincula collo*
> *intendunt; scandit fatalis machina muros*
> *feta armis. pueri circum innuptaeque puellae*
> *sacra canunt funemque manu contingere gaudent;*
> *illa subit mediaeque minans inlabitur urbi.*
> *o patria, o divum domus Ilium et incluta bello*
> *moenia Dardanidum! quater ipso in limine portae*
> *substitit atque utero sonitum quater arma dedere;*
> *instamus tamen immemores caecique furore*
> *et monstrum infelix sacrata sistimus arce.*

(2. 234–245)

We made a breach in the walls and opened up the defences of the city. Everyone fell to the task, and put moving wheels under the feet and attached hempen ropes to its neck: the fateful engine-of-war climbed the walls, filled with armed men. Boys and unmarried girls round about sang hymns and enjoyed touching the rope. It came on and threateningly moved into the centre of the town. Oh my homeland, oh Ilium home of the gods and defences of the people of Dardanus, glorious in war – four times on the very threshold of the gate it came to a stop, and four times the weapons clashed in its belly. But we pressed on without a thought, blind with frenzy, and we set the deadly monster in our holy citadel.

When night falls the armed men descend from the horse, and the slaughter begins. At this point the narrative pauses and Aeneas himself comes into the story. He sees in his sleep a vision of Hector which tells him it is vain to resist. 'If', Hector says, 'Troy could have been defended, my hand would have defended it' (2. 291–292); Aeneas must leave and, taking the images of his gods with him, set up a mighty new city over the sea. This is the very first indication, chronologically, which Aeneas has of his mission and it is interesting to see his reaction to it. He ignores it. He is still the Homeric man, obsessed with the glorious gesture when all is lost, determined to seek death in a last brave and hopeless stand against the enemy. 'Anger and frenzy fire my heart, and my thoughts are that it is glorious to die in battle' (2. 316–317). And again, 'I swear that I did not seek to avoid any weapons or dangers from the Greeks, and I merited death, if that had been my fate' (2. 432–434). He still belongs to the heroic world; he has a long way to go before he can realize that because of his divine mission his life is not his to give away or to live according to his own wishes.

The horror and suffering of this section culminate with the cold-blooded murder of old King Priam:

Haec finis Priami fatorum, hic exitus illum
sorte tulit Troiam incensam et prolapsa videntem
Pergama, tot quondam populis terrisque superbum

29

regnatorem Asiae. iacet ingens litore truncus,
avulsumque umeris caput et sine nomine corpus.

(2. 554–558)

Thus Priam fell, and shared one common fate
With Troy in ashes, and his ruined state:
He who the sceptre of all Asia swayed,
Whom monarchs like domestic slaves obeyed,
On the bleak shore now lies the abandoned king,
A headless carcass and a nameless thing.

(tr. Dryden)

The rest of the book switches to the personal fortunes of
Aeneas and his family, and here too intense tragedy strikes. He
sets out with his father Anchises on his shoulders (after
Anchises has finally been persuaded against his will to leave,
because of divine omens), holding his little son Ascanius by the
hand and with his wife Creusa following behind (this is one of
the favourite themes of all in visual art). In the confusion
Creusa is lost and again Aeneas acts with total disregard for his
personal safety and for the mission which depends on him.
Madly he rushes through the streets held by the victorious
Greeks, calling out Creusa's name – but all in vain. Finally he is
halted by a vision of Creusa; she tells him that it is useless to
seek further, for the mother of the gods herself has Creusa
under her care, and that he is to depart over the sea to found a
kingdom in Hesperia 'where the Lydian Tiber flows with its
gentle stream through the fertile fields' (2. 781–782). Aeneas
recognizes that there is no further hope in Troy, and at first
light he departs to the mountains. The night of Troy is over;
Rome's day dawns.

The Aeneid

The continuation of Aeneas's story to Dido affords a strong
contrast with what went before. Book 2 was intense, immedi-
ate, tragic; Book 3 is diffuse, varied, at an altogether lower level
of emotional intensity. It tells of the long and weary seven-year
voyage in search of the ever-receding shores of Italy. Its interest
is maintained by the theme of the long quest and the gradual
revelation to Aeneas and Anchises of more detail about the
whereabouts of the promised land, and in particular by the
heartening prophecy of future greatness given by the Penates,
the household gods which Aeneas was bringing with him on
his mission:

> *nos te Dardania incensa tuaque arma secuti,*
> *nos tumidum sub te permensi classibus aequor,*
> *idem venturos tollemus in astra nepotes*
> *imperiumque urbi dabimus.*

(3. 156–159)

We have accompanied you and your forces after Troy was
burnt; we have traversed the swelling sea in ships under
your leadership; we shall extol your descendants to the
stars and give empire to your city.

Yet the general tone of the book is one of weariness and
frustration, and it ends with the death of Anchises, leaving
Aeneas alone with his young son to carry out a quest which
seems increasingly beyond human powers of endurance to
fulfil.

Virgil and his Poetry

BOOK 4

Aeneas's story to Dido is complete and we return to the
narrative about Dido's love for him. This book has always been
the most widely read and best-known part of the poem, and the
story of Dido has influenced subsequent literature more than
any other from Roman literature. (Most of the famous myths
of antiquity come from the Greeks, but the Dido we know is
essentially a Virgilian creation.) She is a favourite character in
twelfth- and thirteenth-century French romances; she is in
Chaucer and Shakespeare and Spenser; Marlowe's *Dido Queen
of Carthage* is well-known; and in musical treatments one thinks
immediately of Purcell and Berlioz. She is generally presented
as the innocent victim of fate, or of Aeneas, but Virgil's version
is subtler than that.

Book 1 showed Dido to be wholly admirable; Book 4 tells
the story of her downfall. In the first half we read the account of
her increasing infatuation; she is persuaded by her sister Anna
to break her vow of fidelity to her dead husband Sychaeus, and
she yields wholly to her love. Oblivious of all other considerations than the satisfaction of her love for Aeneas, she abdicates
all her queenly responsibilities and Carthage grinds to a halt.

> *Non coeptae adsurgunt turres, non arma iuventus*
> *exercet portusve aut propugnacula bello*
> *tuta parant: pendent opera interrupta minaeque*
> *murorum ingentes aequataque machina caelo.*

$$(4. 86-89)$$

Meantime the rising towers are at a stand,
No labours exercise the youthful band;
Nor use of arts, nor toils of arms they know,
The mole is left unfinished to the foe;
The mounds, the works, the walls neglected lie,

The Aeneid

Short of their promised height that seemed to threat the sky.

(tr. Dryden)

The scene shifts to heaven where the goddesses Juno and
Venus (each for their own spiteful purposes) plot the further
ensnarement of Dido and arrange a meeting in a cave during a
storm which Dido regards, in her hallucinatory state, as a
marriage. At this stage our sympathy for her is at its height as
she is manipulated by the goddesses, and we ask ourselves
whether any blame can attach to the unhappy queen in these
circumstances. But Virgil has so presented the situation that we
must feel that whatever the pressures on Dido, however
fraught with disaster the situation that has blown up through
no fault of her own, she is nevertheless free at every moment to
try to resist what she knows is wrong (because of her oath to
Sychaeus, and because of her awareness that Aeneas has to go
to Italy and is not free to stay with her). Whether she could
have resisted successfully we do not know – but she was free to
try. She has allowed herself to become enmeshed in a net of
circumstances.

The terms used by Virgil throughout this section to
describe Dido's love for Aeneas are very disquieting – fire,
illness, wounds, frenzy, madness – and when she finally hears
that Aeneas is planning to leave she is compared with a Bacchic
maiden, a devotee of the god Bacchus who has abandoned all
rational control.

It is not till well on into the book that the action centres on
Aeneas. Jupiter sends his messenger to remind Aeneas of his
mission and to ask why he is lingering in Carthage. Aeneas,
like Dido, has forgotten his responsibilities but, unlike her, he
can be recalled to them. He decides immediately that he must
leave and is met by Dido who makes a pleading speech of the
most poignant pathos. She tells him what is only too true – that
she has given up everything for him – and she begs for pity and

protection. It is an appeal which is intensely moving, but Aeneas has to resist it. Suppressing his emotion he tries to show her why he must go, and ends with a brief sentence which summarizes the whole tragic situation: '*Italiam non sponte sequor*'; 'I am making for Italy not because I want to.' Here is the basic human dilemma which Virgil explores in his story of Aeneas and Dido: personal desires are in conflict with duty towards the gods. Aeneas is the kind of person who would choose the second; Dido is the kind who would choose the first. Aeneas has much of the Stoic in him, believing that life should be lived in accordance with the will of heaven; Dido is Epicurean in her outlook, placing the happiness of the individual above everything. At this final moment of their confrontation they cannot appreciate each other's attitude.

It is at this point too that Virgil confronts the meaning of a divine mission: when Aeneas has given so much of himself away to the cause which he feels that he must follow, has he lost his free-will? Has he become a puppet? Virgil's way of telling the story does not suggest so: Aeneas must sacrifice his purely personal wishes, but he does so because he chooses to do so. He could at any time withdraw from his divine mission, but in spite of everything, in spite of the other things he would rather do, he chooses to continue to be a servant of the divine purpose for the world.

Now the final section of the tragedy begins, and we see Dido in quite a different light. She is now no longer the admirable queen of her people, no longer the pathetically doomed lover, but a frightening figure of fury and vengeance. She hurls a series of curses at Aeneas, and swears that she will haunt him after her death and that he will pay the penalty. She plans her suicide and as she sees the Trojans leaving her shores she launches into a terrifying series of curses, first upon Aeneas himself, and finally upon all his descendants. Here are the last lines of her final prayer as she appeals to her people to take after

The Aeneid

her death the vengeance which she cannot take in life:

> *Tum vos, o Tyrii, stirpem et genus omne futurum*
> *exercete odiis, cinerique haec mittite nostro*
> *munera. nullus amor populis nec foedera sunto.*
> *exoriare aliquis nostris ex ossibus ultor*
> *qui face Dardanios ferroque sequare colonos,*
> *nunc, olim, quocumque dabunt se tempore vires.*
> *litora litoribus contraria, fluctibus undas*
> *imprecor, arma armis: pugnent ipsique nepotesque.*
>
> (4. 622–629)

Then you, my Tyrians, harass with hatred his people and all his race to come; make this your offering to my ashes. Let there be no love and no agreement between our peoples. Arise, unknown avenger, from my bones to pursue the Trojan settlers with fire and sword, now, one day, whenever strength offers. I call on shore to fight with shore, wave with sea, weapons with weapons; let the peoples fight, now and to the last generation.

After Dido's suicide the book ends quietly, as a Greek tragedy does, and it is with Greek tragedy that our final thoughts preoccupy themselves. Like the hero or heroine of the great Athenian tragedies of the fifth century BC Dido has insistently walked the path which leads only to the precipice. A great and noble character has come to utter disaster – because of her own fault, or because of the pressure of irresistible circumstances, or because of both?

35

BOOK 5

After the intensity of Book 4, the fifth book (like the third) is at a quieter level. Much of it is taken up with a description of the anniversary games for the death of Anchises a year before, with strong reference to the religious rites involved and duly performed. Here for a little while we see Aeneas with the weight off his shoulders, and it is all the harder for him to bear when suddenly he hears that the Trojan women, weary of the interminable voyage, have set the ships on fire. At Aeneas's prayer Jupiter quenches the fire, but not before four ships are destroyed. Utterly downhearted by this bitter blow Aeneas wonders whether to give up, and this is the place in the poem where his freedom of choice is made most explicit:

> *At pater Aeneas casu concussus acerbo*
> *nunc huc ingentis, nunc illuc pectore curas*
> *mutabat versans, Siculisne resideret arvis*
> *oblitus fatorum, Italasne capesseret oras.*

(5. 700–703)

> But lord Aeneas, shattered by this bitter blow, turned his heavy anxieties this way and that in his heart, weighing them up: should he settle in Sicilian territory and forget the fates, or press on to the shores of Italy?

It needs a vision of his father Anchises to persuade Aeneas to continue, a vision which also instructs him to visit his father in the underworld to learn more of his destiny. (His visit is the subject of the sixth book.) But before Aeneas makes this visit, another disaster strikes: the faithful helmsman Palinurus is swept overboard and lost on the very verge of their arrival in Italy.

The Aeneid

The sixth book, describing Aeneas's descent into the under-world, is the pivot on which the whole poem turns; it concludes the long and weary search for the promised land and provides new impetus for the successful foundation of the new city. Spiritually Aeneas learns to accept what is past and to reach forward towards a future wished for him by the heavenly powers. Something of the mysteries of the afterlife is revealed to him, and much of the future glory of Rome.

The book falls into three sections: the preparations for the descent, the journey through the different parts of the under-world, and finally the meeting in Elysium with the ghost of his father Anchises, and the revelation of the secrets of the afterlife and of Rome's glorious future. The first section builds up an atmosphere of religious awe with the description of the prophetic frenzy of Apollo's priestess, the Sibyl, who is to accompany Aeneas; with the prayers made by Aeneas and the search for the mysterious talisman of the Golden Bough; then with the funeral rites for the sudden death of his companion Misenus, and finally with the last prayers and sacrifices as they enter the underworld at Lake Avernus near Cumae.

At this moment of climax Virgil makes a new invocation:

> *Di, quibus imperium est animarum, umbraeque silentes*
> *et Chaos et Phlegethon, loca nocte tacentia late,*
> *sit mihi fas audita loqui, sit numine vestro*
> *pandere res alta terra et caligine mersas.*
>
> *Ibant obscuri sola sub nocte per umbram*
> *perque domos Ditis vacuas et inania regna:*
> *quale per incertam lunam sub luce maligna*
> *est iter in silvis, ubi caelum condidit umbra*
> *Iuppiter, et rebus nox abstulit atra colorem.*

(6. 264–272)

Virgil and his Poetry

Ye realms yet unrevealed to human sight,
Ye gods who rule the regions of the night,
Ye gliding ghosts, permit me to relate
The mystic wonders of your silent state.
    Obscure they went through dreary shades that led
Along the waste dominions of the dead.
Thus wander travellers in woods by night
By the moon's doubtful and malignant light,
When Jove in dusky clouds involves the skies,
And the faint crescent shoots by fits before their eyes.

(tr. Dryden)

In his description of the journey through the various sections of the underworld, Virgil uses the traditional geography (the river Styx with its ferryman Charon, the dog Cerberus guarding the domain of Pluto, the deepest abyss, Tartarus, for the worst sinners, the final brilliant light of Elysium, land of the blessed) as a background for Aeneas's meetings with the ghosts of his past. He travels again through the traumatic experiences of recent years, meeting first the ghost of Palinurus, so recently lost, then the ghost of Dido for whose suicide he was so largely responsible, and finally the ghost of Deiphobus, his Trojan friend who was killed on Troy's last night when Aeneas escaped. In all these encounters Aeneas is obsessed with feelings of guilt and horror at being reminded of what his mission has already cost in terms of human tragedy. He is backward-looking and deeply depressed. The meeting with Dido in particular is memorable in its intense pathos and reiterates the tragedy of the lovers whose lives could not be joined:

> *Inter quas Phoenissa recens a vulnere Dido*
> *errabat silva in magna; quam Troius heros*
> *ut primum iuxta stetit agnovitque per umbras*

The Aeneid

obscuram, qualem primo qui surgere mense
aut videt aut vidisse putat per nubila lunam,
demisit lacrimas dulcique adfatus amore est:
'infelix Dido, verus mihi nuntius ergo
venerat exstinctam ferroque extrema secutam?
funeris heu tibi causa fui? per sidera iuro,
per superos et si qua fides tellure sub ima est,
invitus, regina, tuo de litore cessi.
sed me iussa deum, quae nunc has ire per umbras,
per loca senta situ cogunt noctemque profundam,
imperiis egere suis; nec credere quivi
hunc tantum tibi me discessu ferre dolorem.
siste gradum teque aspectu ne subtrahe nostro.
quem fugis? extremum fato quod te adloquor hoc est.'
talibus Aeneas ardentem et torva tuentem
lenibat dictis animum lacrimasque ciebat.
illa solo fixos oculos aversa tenebat
nec magis incepto vultum sermone movetur
quam si dura silex aut stet Marpesia cautes.
tandem corripuit sese atque inimica refugit
in nemus umbriferum, coniunx ubi pristinus illi
respondet curis aequatque Sychaeus amorem.
nec minus Aeneas casu percussus iniquo
prosequitur lacrimis longe et miseratur euntem.

(6. 450–476)

Not far from these Phoenician Dido stood,
Fresh from her wound, her bosom bathed in blood,
Whom, when the Trojan hero hardly knew,
Obscure in shades, and with a doubtful view
(Doubtful as he who runs through dusky night,
Or thinks he sees the moon's uncertain light);
With tears he first approached the sullen shade,
And, as his love inspired him, thus he said:

39

Virgil and his Poetry

'Unhappy Queen, then is the common breath
Of rumour true in your reported death?
And I, alas, the cause? By heaven, I vow,
And all the powers that rule the realms below,
Unwilling I forsook your friendly state,
Commanded by the gods and forced by fate –
Those gods, that fate, whose unresisted might
Have sent me to these regions, void of light,
Through the vast empire of eternal night;
Nor dared I to presume that, pressed with grief,
My flight should urge you to this dire relief.
Stay, stay your steps, and listen to my vows –
'Tis the last interview that fate allows!'
In vain he thus attempts her mind to move
With tears and prayers and late repenting love;
Disdainfully she looked, then turning round,
But fixed her eyes unmoved upon the ground,
And what he says and swears regards no more
Than the deaf rocks when the loud billows roar;
But whirled away, to shun his hateful sight,
Hid in the forest and the shades of night;
Then sought Sichaeus through the shady grove,
Who answered all her cares and equalled all her love.
Some pious tears the pitying hero paid,
And followed with his eyes the flitting shade.

(tr. Dryden)

The last section begins with the arrival of Aeneas and the Sibyl in Elysium where they meet the ghost of his father Anchises. He explains to Aeneas something of the secrets of the afterlife, involving purification for sins committed and ultimate paradise for those few whose lives were deserving of it, and rebirth into new bodies, to try again, for the others. This is a religion of hope, in strong contrast with the Homeric underworld which was a wretched shadowy existence in every way inferior to life on earth. Virgil is influenced by Orphic and Stoic ideas and essentially conveys that the injustices and tragedies which apparently cannot be explained in terms of this world will be put right in the world to come. Here are the last two lines of the description of those who reach Elysium:

> *inventas aut qui vitam excoluere per artis,*
> *quique sui memores aliquos fecere merendo.*

> (6. 663–664)

Those who enriched life by finding ways of living it more fully, and those who made people remember them by their kindness.

After the religious explanations Anchises shows his son a pageant of the ghosts of future Roman heroes waiting to be born. They pass before our eyes in splendid array: the kings of Alba, the kings of Rome, the Scipios, Brutus, Caesar, Pompey, and many more; and in the centre, out of chronological order in order to follow Romulus the first king of Rome, is the Emperor Augustus:

> *Hic vir, hic est, tibi quem promitti saepius audis,*
> *Augustus Caesar, divi genus, aurea condet*
> *saecula qui rursus Latio regnata per arva*
> *Saturno quondam, super et Garamantas et Indos*
> *proferet imperium; iacet extra sidera tellus,*
> *extra anni solisque vias, ubi caelifer Atlas*
> *axem umero torquet stellis ardentibus aptum.*
> *huius in adventum iam nunc et Caspia regna*
> *responsis horrent divum et Maeotia tellus,*
> *et septemgemini turbant trepida ostia Nili.*
> *nec vero Alcides tantum telluris obivit,*

41

Virgil and his Poetry

fixerit aeripedem cervam licet, aut Erymanthi
pacarit nemora et Lernam tremefecerit arcu;
nec qui pampineis victor iuga flectit habenis
Liber, agens celso Nysae de vertice tigris.
et dubitamus adhuc virtutem extendere factis,
aut metus Ausonia prohibet consistere terra?   (6. 791–807)

But next behold the youth of form divine,
Caesar himself exalted in his line –
Augustus, promised oft, and long foretold,
Sent to the realm that Saturn ruled of old,
Born to restore a better age of gold.
Afric and India shall his power obey,
He shall extend his propagated sway
Beyond the solar year, without the starry way,
Where Atlas turns the rolling heavens around,
And his broad shoulders with their lights are crowned;
At his foreseen approach already quake
The Caspian kingdoms and Maeotian lake;
Their seers behold the tempest from afar,
And threatening oracles denounce the war;
Nile hears him knocking at his sevenfold gates,
And seeks his hidden spring, and fears his nephew Fates;
Nor Hercules more lands or labours knew,
Not though the brazen-footed hind he slew,
Freed Erymanthus from the foaming boar,
And dipped his arrows in Lernaean gore:
Nor Bacchus, turning from his Indian war,
By tigers drawn triumphant in his car,
From Nisus' top descending on the plains,
With curling vines around his purple reins.
And doubt we yet through dangers to pursue
The paths of honour and a crown in view?

(tr. Dryden)

The Aeneid

Observe the last two lines in this quotation: Anchises knows well the doubts, difficulties, and uncertainties which have beset Aeneas on his mission, and his supernatural revelations serve to strengthen Aeneas's resolution. Finally he sends him back to the upper air after 'firing his heart with love for the glory to come' – *incenditque animum famae venientis amore* (6. 889). This has been the function of Book 6: it has been a sort of spiritual journey in the development of Aeneas's character. Before these revelations he had been hesitant, uncertain, often depressed, not knowing enough of the nature of his calling. Now he is more confident, more resolute, and although there is much more suffering to be endured before his new city can be founded, he goes forth into the rest of his task with new determination and pride.

Virgil and his Poetry

The second half of the *Aeneid* does not contain anything which has captured the imagination of later generations as much as the story of Troy's fall, the tragedy of Dido's suicide, and the mysterious majesty of Aeneas's descent to the underworld. But Virgil himself, as he says in his new invocation (7. 44–45), felt that it was in some way the greater and more important part of his poem. Why should he have thought this?

The subject matter of the second half concerns the arrival of the Trojans in Italy and the war which they are forced to fight because of the hostility, inspired by Juno, of the Italians and especially of their leader Turnus. Deeds of valour are performed on both sides, tragic deaths come upon Italian and Trojan warriors alike, and at the end the outcome is determined by Aeneas's victory over Turnus in single combat. The material of the narrative lacks the variety and the imaginative intensity of the first half. What then does it offer?

Essentially the second half is about the nature of war, its heroisms, its tragedies, its apparent inevitability in the Roman world, above all its folly. The Italians against whom the Trojans fought were at first ready to welcome their foreign visitors, but they were stirred to armed resistance by the machinations of Juno. They were destined to make a much greater contribution to the future of the Roman people than their Trojan conquerors, and yet they fought tooth and nail against this destiny. At the height of the battle, in a new invocation, Virgil asks, 'Was it really your pleasure, Jupiter, that peoples destined to live together in the future in peace should fight each other so violently?' (12. 503–54).

Recent Roman history greatly coloured Virgil's description of the fighting. The almost constant series of civil wars in the last years of the Republic had caused deep feelings of guilt in the Roman world and Virgil's handling of his legendary material reflects these feelings. Aeneas does in warfare what has to be done, but he is generally deeply unhappy about it.

There is also a strong literary background to these scenes of warfare. Homer's *Iliad* is largely concerned with fighting, and the second half of the *Aeneid* is Virgil's *Iliad*, as the first half had been his *Odyssey*. But the treatment of the battle scenes in Virgil is different from that of the *Iliad*. Episode after episode recalls Homeric events, but the mood and tone of the writing is different. Homer's *Iliad* indeed depicts with power and sympathy the destruction and sufferings of warfare, but in a context which does not question them. They are recorded as an inevitable part of the environment of the heroic world. Virgil's descriptions of violent death, often as horrific – and sometimes more so – than Homer's, are presented in such a way as to seem unacceptable. His Rome had grown great because of military might, and the greatness of Rome was part of the divine plan for mankind, and yet – 'Was it really your pleasure, Jupiter . . .?'

This, then, is the dilemma which the second half of the *Aeneid* explores: a mission to found Rome, on which Aeneas is the agent of heaven's wishes, meets with violent opposition – often not really intended by those who were caught up in it; how is Aeneas, who wants peace, to deal with this violent opposition? Let us look at some of the episodes which Virgil chooses in his exploration of mankind at war.

There is no sign of the disasters to come in the first part of Book 7: the Trojans arrive at the Tiber and are welcomed by King Latinus, who recognizes the fulfilment of an oracle that foreigners will come to intermarry with the Latins and found a great empire. He promises Aeneas his daughter Lavinia in marriage. This happy state of affairs is shattered by the intervention of Juno, who arouses frenzied anger in Turnus, a local chieftain who was a suitor of Lavinia, and in Queen Amata, who favoured Turnus's suit. Next Juno organizes an incident to spark off the fighting, and personally opens the Gates of War. Virgil invites us to consider to what extent external malevolent forces (personified as Juno) are responsible, and to what extent existing feelings of anger and hatred in Turnus and Amata are symbolized in the goddess.

The war, then, has broken out; but now the action is held in suspense, first by a catalogue of military forces. This was an expected part of an epic poem, the precedent for it having been set in Homer with his catalogue of the Greek ships (*Iliad* 2), but Virgil has made a characteristic alteration in the tradition, in that his catalogue is of the enemy forces, the Italians. We are made to feel unsure which side we are on.

Throughout the whole of Book 8 the military action is still suspended. The book deals with Aeneas's visit to Evander, King of Pallanteum, a little settlement on the site of the seven hills upon which one day Rome would be founded. Aeneas is shown the familiar landmarks of the Rome of Virgil's day, and is promised the help of a contingent of forces to be led by Evander's young son Pallas. The book ends with a description of the pictures on the new shield which Vulcan makes for Aeneas. Again this is a traditional feature of epic poetry, based on Homer's description in *Iliad* 18 of the new shield which Hephaestus makes for Achilles, but again Virgil has altered his model. The motivation for Achilles's new shield is totally logical: his original shield has been lost (having been lent to Patroclus), and so Homer takes the opportunity of describing the new one. In Virgil there is no such logical reason why Aeneas should have a new shield; Virgil simply wants to give us pictures of great moments in Roman history at this point in the poem, just before the violent battles commence in full scale. We must be reminded once more why blood must flow, why brave warriors must die. We still may not feel that it is acceptable, but Rome's greatness is the only justification and it must be shown to us in all its glory here. The centre-piece of the shield is the battle of Actium with Augustus defeating Antony and Cleopatra. The battles which Aeneas must now fight lead in a thousand years to the foundation of the Roman Empire and the hopes that from that time wars would be finally laid aside.

> *Talia per clipeum Volcani, dona parentis,*
> *miratur rerumque ignarus imagine gaudet*
> *attollens umero famamque et fata nepotum.* (8. 729–731)

Such were the scenes at which Aeneas marvelled on the shield which Vulcan had made, the gift of his mother Venus; and ignorant of what they were he rejoiced in the pictures of these events as he raised on to his shoulders the glory and the destiny of his descendants.

In the ninth book the battles begin, and continue with little intermission to the end of the poem. In the absence of Aeneas Turnus attacks the Trojan camp, and the impression that we already have received of his character is reinforced as he shows his courage, his impetuous reactions, his reckless self-confidence. He appears very clearly as a hero of the Homeric mould, another Achilles, bold, individualistic, determined above all else to display his prowess and defend his honour. In many ways he commands our sympathy, perhaps largely because he is such an uncomplicated character who knows what he should do and to the best of his ability sets out directly to do it. But at the end of the book, when he is carried away by his success to the extent that he thinks he can win the war on his own, we feel that he is lacking in judgement, that for him glory outweighs everything. He is in strong contrast with Aeneas; he seems set on personal aggrandizement, while Aeneas has constantly to sacrifice his own personality to the requirements of his duty.

47

Virgil and his Poetry

This impression is greatly strengthened by the events of Book 10. Aeneas returns, the young Pallas joins the fighting on the Trojan side, and Turnus immediately makes for Pallas.

> *Ut vidit socios: 'tempus desistere pugnae;*
> *solus ego in Pallanta feror, soli mihi Pallas*
> *debetur; cuperem ipse parens spectator adesset.'*
>
> (10. 441–443)

> And making to his friends, thus calls aloud:
> 'Let none presume his needless aid to join;
> Retire, and clear the field, the fight is mine.
> To this right hand is Pallas only due.
> Oh, were his father here my just revenge to view!'
>
> (tr. Dryden)

In the unequal contest Pallas is killed, and Turnus, boasting over him, says:

> *'Arcades, haec' inquit 'memores mea dicta referte*
> *Euandro: qualem meruit, Pallanta remitto.*
> *quisquis honos tumuli, quidquid solamen humandi est,*
> *largior. haud illi stabunt Aeneia parvo*
> *hospitia.'*
>
> (10. 491–495)

> Turnus bestrode the corse: 'Arcadians, hear,'
> Said he; 'my message to your master bear:
> "Such as the sire deserved, the son I send;
> It costs him dear to be the Phrygian's friend."'
>
> (tr. Dryden)

Whatever sympathy we may have had for Turnus evaporates here, and Virgil emphasizes the effect his narrative has already had upon us by a device, rare in epic poetry, of intervening personally in his narrative:

> *nescia mens hominum fati sortisque futurae*
> *et servare modum rebus sublata secundis!*
> *Turno tempus erit magno cum optaverit emptum*
> *intactum Pallanta, et cum spolia ista diemque*
> *oderit.*
>
> (10. 501–505)

> O mortals, blind in fate, who never know
> To bear high fortune, or endure the low!
> The time shall come when Turnus, but in vain,
> Shall wish untouched the trophies of the slain –
> Shall wish the fatal belt were far away,
> And curse the dire remembrance of the day.
>
> (tr. Dryden)

As we shall see, this passage anticipates the scene at the poem's end.

Now the narrative switches to Aeneas. We feel at this point that we know the kind of man Turnus is in battle; we are shocked to find that Aeneas, when he learns of Pallas's death, becomes the same kind of man. He is not so normally, but now, under the stress of his cruel grief, he behaves in every way as savagely as Turnus had. He goes berserk on the battlefield, mowing down all who stand in his way, taunting them cruelly as they die, hearing no pleas for mercy but sating his anger in blood. Is this the first ancestor of the Roman Empire, whose proud boast was to bring peace to the world and spare the conquered? For the moment it is.

It is not long before revulsion overcomes Aeneas. Young Lausus tries to defend his father against Aeneas's onslaught, and Aeneas kills him. As he does so, he thinks of how he would have defended his own father, and in sorrow and anguish he picks up the body of the youth he has slaughtered, and returns it to his comrades. There is in these battle-scenes of the tenth book a deep inconsistency in Aeneas: he is one kind of man in one situation, and another in another. He reflects Virgil's own experience of Roman life in his day.

The eleventh book begins with Aeneas behaving again as we expect him to – sorrowing at the funeral of Pallas, proclaiming his hatred of war, and wishing to grant mercy to his adversaries. At the end of Pallas's funeral he says:

> '*Nos alias hinc ad lacrimas eadem horrida belli fata vocant:*
> *salve aeternum mihi, maxime Palla, aeternumque vale.*'
>
> (11. 96–98)

> 'These same grim fates of war call us from here to other
> tears: hail for ever, I say, mighty Pallas, and for ever
> farewell.'

Then, when spokesmen come from the enemy asking for a truce to bury the dead, he replies in a way which we feel expresses his true attitude when reason and not passion is governing him:

> *pacem me exanimis et Martis sorte peremptis*
> *oratis? equidem et vivis concedere vellem.*
>
> (11. 110–111)

> You beg a truce, which I would gladly give,
> Not only for the slain, but those who live.
>
> (tr. Dryden)

The scene now switches back to Turnus, and we see him in debate, defending his determination to destroy the Trojans.

The Aeneid

Again it is made evident that he is motivated by personal honour and pride in his prowess. War-scenes are again prominent, centring on one of Turnus's chief allies, the warrior-maid Camilla. When she is killed the Latin forces fall back in retreat, and the final book of the *Aeneid* begins with everything depending on Turnus.

> *Turnus ut infractos adverso Marte Latinos*
> *defecisse videt, sua nunc promissa reposci,*
> *se signari oculis, ultro implacabilis ardet*
> *attollitque animos.*
>
> (12. 1–4)

When Turnus saw that the Latins were broken and defeated by the disaster in the battle, and that now his promises were looked for, that he was the cynosure of all eyes, then instantly he blazed with implacable fury and his spirit was exalted.

He is like a wounded lion at bay – he welcomes the challenge of settling the issue by single combat with Aeneas, he rejects the pleas of the king and the queen, and he arms himself in preparation, rejoicing in handling his weapons, his eyes sparkling in anticipation. Fighting is what he can do superbly well, and he is ready to do it – even against these odds. Preparations are made for the single combat, and oaths are sworn: Aeneas promises that if he loses he will leave the territory, and that if he wins he will not seek dominion over the Italians, but both peoples shall unite under equal laws. However, the Rutulian soldiers are filled with shame at committing their fortunes to what they feel is an unequal combat and they break the truce; general fighting begins again. Aeneas acts as we would expect: he tries to stop the renewal of hostilities.

Virgil and his Poetry

At pius Aeneas dextram tendebat inermem
nudato capite atque suos clamore vocabat:
'quo ruitis? quaeve ista repens discordia surgit?
o cohibete iras! ictum iam foedus et omnes
compositae leges. mihi ius concurrere soli.'

(12. 311–315)

But good Aeneas rushed amid the bands,
Bare was his head and naked were his hands
In sign of truce. Then thus he cries aloud:
'What sudden rage, what new desire of blood
Inflames your altered minds? O Trojans, cease
From impious arms, nor violate the peace.
By human sanctions and by laws divine,
The terms are all agreed, the war is mine.'

(tr. Dryden)

His peace-making efforts are interrupted as a chance arrow wounds him. The wound is supernaturally healed, but it has been enough to cause Aeneas to lose control of himself (as he had when Pallas was killed) and again he rages in mad fury over the battlefield. Turnus does the same in a different part of the fighting, and as the slaughter wrought by the two leaders is described we feel that there is hardly any difference between them.

By divine intervention on Juno's part Turnus is kept away from the crucial area of the fighting, and in his absence the Trojans surround the walls of the Latin capital. The queen commits suicide and Turnus becomes aware that his chariot is being driven not by his charioteer, but by his disguised sister, who with Juno's aid is keeping him away from trouble. At this realization he takes on a new heroic stature as he faces up to the inevitable, and our sympathy swings towards him:

The Aeneid

Terga dabo et Turnum fugientem haec terra videbit?
usque adeone mori miserum est? vos o mihi, Manes,
este boni, quoniam superis aversa voluntas.
sancta ad vos anima atque istius inscia culpae
descendam magnorum haud umquam indignus avorum.

(12. 645–649)

Is death so hard to bear? ye gods below
(Since those above so small compassion show),
Receive a soul unsullied yet with shame,
Which not belies my great forefathers' name.

(tr. Dryden)

He hears the news of the siege of the capital and the queen's
suicide, and is bemused like the hero of a Greek tragedy whom
the blows of fate have battered into helplessness:

obstipuit varia confusus imagine rerum
Turnus et obtutu tacito stetit; aestuat ingens
uno in corde pudor mixtoque insania luctu
et furiis agitatus amor et conscia virtus.

(12. 665–668)

Stupid he sate, his eyes on earth declined,
And various cares revolving in his mind;
Rage boiling from the bottom of his breast,
And sorrow mixed with shame his soul oppressed,
And conscious worth lay labouring in his thought,
And love by jealousy to madness wrought.

(tr. Dryden)

The single combat between the two opposing leaders now
begins, but it is suspended in mid-narrative as Virgil takes us
for the last time away from the earthly scene to the halls of

53

Virgil and his Poetry

Olympus where Jupiter and Juno confront each other. This is an immensely important scene in the poem, and Virgil highlights it by its position just before the outcome of the duel between Aeneas and Turnus. Jupiter tells Juno that he forbids her to intervene any further against the Trojans. She yields – as she now must – to the requirements of Fate, but she begs Jupiter for three conditions to be granted: that the people who will be descended from the intermixing of the Trojans and Italians should still be called Latins (not Trojans), that they should still speak Latin, and that they should not change their manner of dress. Magnificently she implores: 'Let the Roman offspring be strong because of Italian qualities.' Jupiter grants her requests, indeed enlarges them, changing 'manner of dress' to the much broader phrase 'way of life'. Juno, then, is responsible for the historical situation of Virgil's time when the Romans were of course far more Italian than Trojan (in the description of the battle of Actium, Augustus leads the *Italians* into battle, 8. 678); and we see now at last some sort of justification for all the horror and disaster caused by Juno. In a way which the mortal mind cannot understand, human suffering somehow leads to a good outcome. Virgil does not say this explicitly, but it is the nearest he gets to answering the question which he posed at the beginning of the poem – why do gods cause suffering? It is not only that humans are toughened by it, but also that the suffering itself may actually lead to a desirable end.

Now we come to the last scene of all, and an astonishing scene it is. All through the single combat we have been reminded, by striking resemblances of episode and phraseology, of the most famous single combat in Greek literature, that between Achilles and Hector in *Iliad* 22. It was motivated in the same way, by the death of Patroclus in Homer as of Pallas in Virgil, and we feel that we are watching the well-known chase in reverse, with the Achilles figure (Turnus) this time in the losing situation. When Aeneas wounds Turnus and he begs for mercy, we suddenly realize the point of difference that will emerge from all these similarities. Our victorious hero will not behave like Achilles, who in a savage speech refused mercy to Hector, but he will be true to the ideal which he has been trying to realize throughout the poem – the Roman ideal of 'combatting the proud, and sparing the conquered'. Turnus has indeed been proud – the word *superbus* has often been used of him – but when he is wounded and makes his plea he is called *humilis*, 'humble', the opposite of proud, and therefore we are sure that he will be spared. It comes as a savage shock when Aeneas does not spare him, but kills his helpless suppliant in a fit of frenzied anger in order to exact vengeance for Pallas. And the poem ends not with a note of triumph that the last obstacle to the fulfilment of the Roman mission has been removed, but with a sad sentence about the death of Turnus:

> *Ast illi solvuntur frigore membra*
> *vitaque cum gemitu fugit indignata sub umbras.*   (12. 951–952)

But Turnus's limbs were loosened in the chill of death, and his life with a groan departed complaining to the world below.

What are we to make of this? The most obvious reaction is amazement that a man who has struggled to show rational control and mercy whenever he could throughout the poem should so disgrace himself at the end. But another thought comes too – was it disgraceful? When Turnus slaughtered Pallas in Book 10, we were led to believe that Turnus must pay for it. Now he pays – and we do not like it. Also, Augustus had vowed he would not rest until he had hunted out and taken vengeance on all the assassins of Julius Caesar; he had done so, and later built a temple to 'Mars the Avenger' in his forum. So are we to approve of Aeneas's act? The answer must be no, we are not. Virgil has presented it as a sad and perplexing end to his poem. Human behaviour in the Roman *Aeneid* has not changed in this respect from the heroic times of Homer – perhaps it should have done, but Virgil does not feel that it has, and the poem finishes with a sense of uncertainty and dilemma. Virgil wants his Roman reader to feel that if he thinks he knows the answers he probably has not understood the questions. In a passage of extraordinary intensity Virgil has shown that man's compassion may be outweighed by instinctive emotional reaction; and while he may imply that it should not be so, he does not pretend, in order to produce a specious and comfortable ending to the poem, that it is not so.

4

VIRGIL TODAY

Perhaps more than any other Roman writer, Virgil has expressed the achievements, and the shortcomings, of that civilization of which we are the children, in a way that has led to his being called 'the father of the western world'. But supposing that we were not his children, supposing that we were people from Mars freshly arrived on this planet and able to read Latin, would we find in him qualities to ensure his continued survival? I think that we would.

Those qualities that make Virgil's poetry relevant today, two thousand years after his death, can be assessed by looking at two main aspects of a poet's work: technical skills in poetic craftsmanship, and the exploration of the underlying meanings and potentialities of human existence.

Technical skills mean the ability to use words in poetic composition – as a carpenter uses wood or a potter clay or an architect space – to produce something which has an aesthetic impact by its mastery of technique. The most obvious of these skills is the ability to produce word-music – 'the sweetness of the sound' as Dryden called it – and here it has been universally agreed, even by those few who have been unreceptive towards him otherwise, that Virgil was pre-eminent. He was helped in this by having available as the appropriate metre for epic poetry the Latin hexameter, adapted from Greek by Ennius, and developed by Cicero, Catullus, Lucretius, and others, until in

Virgil and his Poetry

Virgil's hand it became what Tennyson called 'the stateliest measure ever moulded by the lips of man'. The full elaboration of this would involve a lengthy technical discussion, and suffice it to say here that Virgil explored to the full the sonorous beauty of the Latin language so that the sound of his words could echo, and indeed express, the sense of the meaning. In particular the nature of the hexameter (a metre based on quantity) and the pronunciation of Latin (based like English on accent) gave two rhythms which could be employed in harmony or counterpoint as the mood and sense required.

This sense of word-music contributed greatly to a second technical requirement in poetry, descriptive power, and Virgil's word-music was supported by his almost unique imaginative visualization. He loved to depict scenes which the human eye does not see: the imaginary Golden Age in *Eclogues* 4, Orpheus and Eurydice in the underworld in *Georgics* 4, the Olympian gods in the *Aeneid* going about their business in the halls of heaven. We see this kind of skill right at the beginning of the *Aeneid* in the mythological description of the winds imprisoned in Aeolus's mountain:

> *Hic vasto rex Aeolus antro*
> *luctantis ventos tempestatesque sonoras*
> *imperio premit ac vinclis et carcere frenat.*
> *illi indignantes magno cum murmure montis*
> *circum claustra fremunt: celsa sedet Aeolus arce*
> *sceptra tenens mollitque animos et temperat iras;*
> *ni faciat, maria ac terras caelumque profundum*
> *quippe ferant rapidi secum verrantque per auras.*
>
> (*Aeneid* 1. 52–59)

Where in a spacious cave of living stone,
The tyrant Aeolus from his airy throne,
With power imperial curbs the struggling winds,

Virgil Today

And sounding tempests in dark prisons binds.
This way and that the impatient captives tend,
And pressing for release, the mountains rend:
High in his hall the undaunted monarch stands,
And shakes his sceptre, and their rage commands;
Which did he not, their unresisted sway
Would sweep the world before them in their way:
Earth, air, and seas through empty space would roll,
And Heaven would fly before the driving soul.

(tr. Dryden)

This sort of imaginative description colours the whole of the *Aeneid*. We are invited to visualize Juno striding majestically through the halls of heaven, Jupiter smiling at his daughter Venus, Neptune driving over the sea in his chariot with his retinue of strange sea-deities, Iris descending to heaven on her own rainbow:

> *Ergo Iris croceis per caelum roscida pennis*
> *mille trahens varios adverso sole colores*
> *devolat.*

(Aeneid 4. 700–702)

Downward the various goddess took her flight,
And drew a thousand colours from the light.

(tr. Dryden)

The Olympian gods in Virgil play many parts in the *Aeneid* as well as the purely descriptive, but it would be a mistake to underestimate Virgil's delight in painting these pictures. In Book 2 Venus shows to her son the divinities of Olympus working the destruction of Troy, which she can see and he cannot: here is Neptune with his mighty trident uprooting the walls of Troy, here is Juno holding the Scaean

59

Gate, here is Pallas on the citadel, and Jupiter himself giving strength to the Greeks. 'Look', Venus tells Aeneas, 'for I will take from you all the cloud which now veils your sight and blunts your mortal vision, darkening your eyes with its mist.' We may think of Virgil as doing for us what Venus does for her son – showing us through his poetic vision what otherwise we could not see. Anyone who loves pictures must love Virgil.

Another essential technical skill for an epic poet is the ability to tell a story in an exciting way. In this respect Virgil is often compared unfavourably with Homer, and most people would agree that in sheer narrative speed and excitement Homer takes the palm. Virgil's epic method (like Milton's) is different, but that is not to say that he does not hold us with bated breath on occasion; for example, the story in Book 2 of the wooden horse, the treachery of Sinon, the last hours of Troy, moves with a verve which is breathtaking.

One might continue with other instances of technical skill in poetry, for example, Virgil's use of brilliant rhetoric in speeches. Those between Turnus and Drances, or especially between the goddesses Juno and Venus, enable us to relax emotionally, and enjoy intellectually the brilliant firework display of exaggerated oratory, in which Cicero would have revelled.

Or again we might consider the structure of Virgil's poetry. The *Eclogues* are symmetrically and elegantly organized in the Alexandrian mode, sometimes with balancing verses from two competitors in a song contest, sometimes with repeated refrain. The first two and the last two books of the *Georgics* cohere in their content, but in mood Books 1 and 3 correspond, and Books 2 and 4. Descriptive passages throughout are interspersed with didactic information in order to give variety of structure. The *Aeneid* especially shows architectural construction on a large scale. This is clearly a requirement of epic above all other kinds of poetry: the epic poet must be a builder on a large scale, able to handle his masses of material. Symmetries and contrasts may be seen between the two halves of the poem, between the first third and the last third, between the different books, and between the different sections of each book. Much has been written about Virgil's skill in structure during recent years, so much so that one should enter a *caveat* and say that however important the structure of poetry may be, it differs from architecture in that structure should be subservient to the poetic message; it is not an end in itself.

This brings us to the second main aspect of a poet's work: the underlying significance of the poetry in relation to human experience. The message conveyed by means of technical skills is obviously deeper in some poets than in others. Most of us could name poets whom we greatly enjoy solely or very largely because of the technical skills just mentioned, and we derive aesthetic rather than intellectual pleasure from their poetry. Virgil, however, is one of those poets who used his aesthetic skills not only for their own sakes, but in order to explore human behaviour in its most crucial aspects.

In the *Eclogues* some critics have put their greatest emphasis on the pure loveliness of the poetry, but increasingly in modern times these poems have been seen as explorations of an idyllic world to which mankind could attain but from which he may be excluded by the social and political pressures of real life. The fourth *Eclogue* is a vision of such a golden world; the first and ninth show the agony of the loss, through dispossession, of the happiness which the idyllic countryside offers. Here is a part of the first *Eclogue*, conveying the envy of the dispossessed for the shepherd who still retains his pastoral world:

> *fortunate senex, hic inter flumina nota*
> *et fontis sacros frigus captabis opacum;*
> *hinc tibi quae semper vicino ab limite saepes*
> *Hyblaeis apibus florem depasta salicti*

Virgil and his Poetry

saepe levi somnum suadebit inire susurro;
hinc alta sub rupe canet frondator ad auras:
nec tamen interea raucae, tua cura, palumbes
nec gemere aeria cessabit turtur ab ulmo.

(*Eclogues* 1. 51–58)

Ah, fortunate old man, here among hallowed springs
And familiar streams you'll enjoy the longed-for shade,
   the cool shade.
Here, as of old, where your neighbour's land marches with yours,
The sally hedge, with bees of Hybla sipping its blossom,
Shall often hum you gently to sleep. On the other side
Vine-dressers will sing to the breezes at the crag's foot;
And all the time your favourites, the husky-voiced wood pigeons
Shall coo away, and turtle doves make moan in the elm tops.

(tr. Day Lewis)

The *Georgics* too have had, and still have, a great appeal
purely because of their descriptive power, and the best-known
parts have always been the most brilliant of the descriptive
passages, like the praises of Italy (2. 136ff.) or the activities of
the bees (4. 67ff.). But again modern criticism has concentrated
on the concept in the poem of man as part of nature, divinely
created, and on his successes and failures. The poem is seen as a
presentation of the positive achievements of man in fitting
himself in to the world of nature, and of the disasters which
sometimes seem inexplicable (like flood or fire or the plague)
and which sometimes are due to man's own folly in the neglect
of his duty towards 'the divine countryside'. Above all the life
of the countryman is extolled as a religious communion with
nature, calling for 'unremitting toil' and resilience, but offering
the richest of rewards. Here is a passage contrasting the
ambitious, wealth-seeking town-dweller with the contented
farmer:

Virgil Today

condit opes alius defossoque incubat auro;
hic stupet attonitus rostris, hunc plausus hiantem
per cuneos geminatus enim plebisque patrumque
corripuit; gaudent perfusi sanguine fratrum,
exsilioque domos et dulcia limina mutant
atque alio patriam quaerunt sub sole iacentem.
agricola incurvo terram dimovit aratro:
hic anni labor, hinc patriam parvosque nepotes
sustinet, hinc armenta boum meritosque iuvencos.

(Georgics 2. 507–515)

One piles up great wealth, gloats over his cache of gold;
One gawps at the public speakers; one is worked up to hysteria
By the plaudits of senate and people resounding across the benches:
These shed their brothers' blood
Merrily, they barter for exile their homes beloved
And leave for countries lying under an alien sun.
  But still the farmer furrows the land with his
      curving plough:
The land is his annual labour, it keeps his native country,
His little grandsons and herds of cattle and trusty bullocks.

(tr. Day Lewis)

The *Aeneid* differs from the *Eclogues* and the *Georgics* with regard to its underlying significance in that it deals with man's problems by presenting and developing individual characters in constantly changing situations. The characters of the *Eclogues* are in a sense static pictures in a given situation; the characters of the *Georgics* (except for the Orpheus and Eurydice story) are not individuals at all, but generalized types. The *Aeneid*, however, as is appropriate for an epic poem, dwells at length on character, and this is best illustrated by focussing on the hero of the poem.

First and foremost Aeneas is a man who has accepted a

divine mission which dictates the whole of his actions. He would have preferred to die at Troy among his friends, he would have preferred to stay with Dido, but because he has received intimations by means of visions, dreams and oracles that he has been chosen as the agent of Providence to fulfil a destiny which will bring great benefits to mankind, he devotes himself to this mission. Throughout the poem Virgil explores the effect which such a calling has upon an individual, and many readers of the *Aeneid* have thought that it causes Aeneas to be a puppet-like creature in whose activities it is hard to take an interest. This is a wholly mistaken view: he is in fact free at any time to cry 'Enough', to decide that his mission is too hard or too uncertain or too unconvincing for him to continue. That he does continue – often by the skin of his teeth – is due to a series of acts of his own free-will. This is explicitly shown, as we have seen, in a passage already referred to (5. 700–703) where he ponders on two possible courses of action: continuing with his mission, or abandoning it, 'forgetting' the fates. Thus the fascination of Aeneas lies in the character study of a man whose actions are guided by a sense of divine duty, which he has to struggle to obey, falteringly at first but then with increasing confidence as he becomes more aware of the nature of his calling. Throughout the poem he is devoutly religious in prayer and sacrifice, but increasingly he begins to understand God's purpose for the world and his part in it.

This devotion to the divine will, involving often the sacrifice of personal wishes, covers a large part of Virgil's frequent epithet for Aeneas – *pius*, 'devoted', 'ready to accept responsibility', 'aware of his duty'. But there are other aspects of this specially Roman virtue which affect his actions. Patriotism is one, and in Aeneas's case this merges with his devotion to the gods whose intention it is to found the Roman race. Care for his family is another, and this is a powerful motivation for his actions. He saves his father from the burning ruins of Troy, and pays the utmost attention to his advice until the very moment of his death. His concern for his son Iulus is evident throughout, and his last words to him are the poignant ones:

Disce, puer, virtutem ex me verumque laborem,
fortunam ex aliis.

(12. 435–436)

Learn, my son, valour from me and the reality of toil,
but good luck from others.

Care for his friends and his fellow-soldiers is a part of *pietas*, and here again Aeneas does all he can to safeguard his followers (unlike Turnus, whose rash impetuousness leads to many unnecessary deaths). Aeneas is the group hero, the social man.

To achieve this object (which he does not always succeed in doing) Aeneas has to sacrifice something of himself – he gives away something of his own personal individuality in the interests of his duty. In this he contrasts with the vivid personalities of Homer's heroes; they shine more brightly than Aeneas because they are always themselves, seeing life very clearly, understanding their obligations clearly, but not having to struggle inwardly with themselves in order to try to determine the right course of action. They know instinctively what the right course is, and to the best of their ability they set about doing it. But Aeneas is always groping for a way of life which he does not fully understand, and in the course of it tragedies and disasters befall him and others for which he feels guiltily responsible. In a paradoxical way it is his *pietas* which is responsible for the cruelty with which he treats Dido (indeed Virgil implies as much, 4. 393): he sacrifices his own personal wishes (and with them hers) to what he sees to be a higher responsibility.

Virgil and his Poetry

In contrast with Aeneas both Dido and Turnus are characters drawn very simply, on Homeric lines. Dido knows exactly what she wants, and is not swayed from her personal desire by any other considerations at all. Her duty towards the city of Carthage is forgotten and she alienates her subjects by her disregard of all her queenly duties. She is completely unable to understand Aeneas's arguments that he would like to stay with her but cannot; for her 'like to' and 'can' are the same. Similarly, Turnus is not confused in his attitude by any attempt to weigh up the requirements of Fate, or the wishes of his king, against his own personal determination to have his own way if he possibly can. With both Dido and Turnus we feel that they have been treated scurvily by the force of events – but they are neither of them prepared to compromise in any way with what they want to do.

Aeneas for the most part is very different – thinking always of the implications of a situation and often deciding to act against his own personal wishes. But there are moments when he loses this rational control and lets himself be swayed by his personal instincts – as when he hears of the death of Pallas in Book 10 and rages wildly over the battle-field dealing indiscriminate slaughter; or again after he has been wounded in Book 12; or finally at the end of the poem when he kills Turnus in hot anger. The last adjective to be applied to him in the poem is *fervidus*, 'in a passion'. In founding Rome he has not trodden an easy path, and he has left it bestrewn with the corpses of those who wished to help as well as those who wished to hinder.

Very many critics in the two thousand years of the *Aeneid*'s existence have found it above all a poem of sadness, of the world's tragedies, of this our vale of sorrow, and Virgil is often thought of as the poet of the 'tears in things', *lacrimae rerum*. To a very large extent this is true; and yet the vision of a Roman Empire spreading peace and civilization to a war-weary world never fades altogether, and in the attempts of Aeneas, very imperfect though they are, to set in motion the beginnings of this worldly paradise we see something of mankind's indomitable spirit, through mistakes and setbacks and calamities, to press onwards: 'to strive, to seek, to find, and not to yield'.

THE PLATES

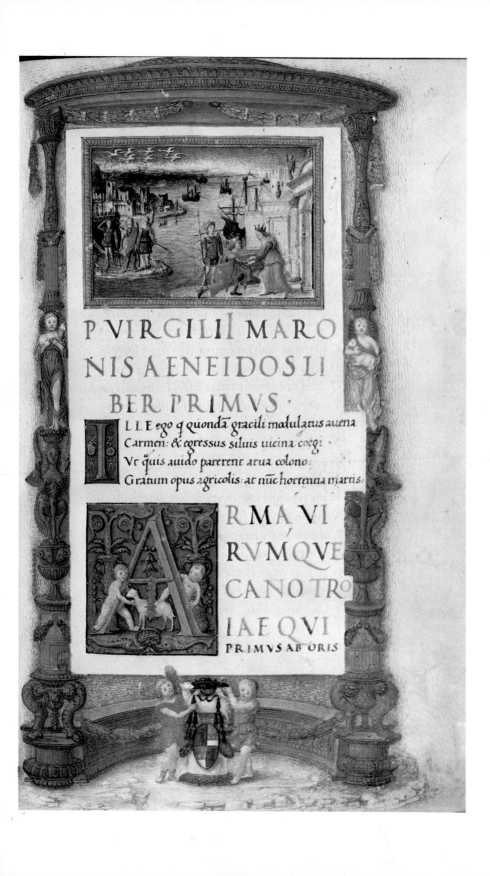

I umperi grauis umbra nocet et frugib umbra
A te domum saturæ uenit hesperus ite capellae,
P. MARONI VIRGILII MATVANI DIVI POETAE BV
COLICO2 LIBER EXPLICIT. SEQVT GEORGICA.

id faciat lætas segetes quo sidere terram
Vertere mecenas ulmis
q; adiungere uites
Conueniat quæ cura
bouum qs cultus huido
it pecori; atq; apibus quanta expientia pcis
Hinc cance incipiam, uos o clarissima mudi
Lumina labentem cælo quæ ducitis annu
Liber et alma ceres uro si munere tellus
Chaoniam pingui glandem mutauit arista,
Poculaq; inuentis acheloia miscuit uuis,
Et uos agrestum præsentia numina faum
Ferte simul satyriq; pedem dryadesq; puellae'
Munera ura cano. tuq; o cui prima fremete
Fudit equm magno tellus percussa tridenti
Heptune; et cultor nemoru cui pinguia cex
Tercentum niuei tondent dumeta iuuenci
Ipe nemus linquens patriu saltusq; lycei

ABOVE: *Eclogue 3*, 262–316, from a 10th-century manuscript, one of the earliest Virgils in the British Library; the dark patches show where the silver has oxidised. (Harley MS 3072 f.1b; British Library)

LEFT: The beginning of the *Georgics*, from a 15th-century Italian manuscript. The full border includes two charming dragons in the upper part and incorporates the tail of the sumptuous 'Q' initial. (Add. MS 14815 f.17b; British Library)

LEFT: Roman pottery lamp, 1st century AD, showing the shepherd Tityrus; his name is the first word of the *Eclogues* and it has sometimes been claimed that he represents Virgil himself. (British Museum)

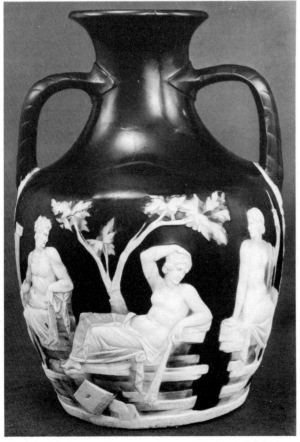

RIGHT: Roman silver cups, contemporary with Virgil. That below shows a mythological scene; that above shows some of the plants described by Virgil in the *Georgics*. (British Museum)

LEFT: The Portland Vase, 1st century BC, depicting the marriage of Peleus and Thetis; an example of superb Roman artistry in Virgil's period. (British Museum)

Woodcut by Sebastian Brant illustrating the *Georgics*, from *Works of Virgil*, published by Johannes Grüninger at Strasbourg in 1502. (Mansell Collection)

Ducat & intacta totidem cervice iuvencas
Post ubi nona suos aurora induxerat ortus
Inferias orphei mittit lucumq reuisat
Hic uero subitum ac dictu mirabile monstrum
Aspiciunt liquefacta boum per uiscera toto
Stridere apes utero & ruptis efferuere costis
Immensasq trahi nubes iamq arbore summa
Confluere & lentis uua demittere ramis
Haec super aruorum cultu pecorumq canebam
Et super arboribus caesar dum magnus ad altum
Fulminat euphraten bello uictorq uolentis
Per populos dat iura uiamq affectat olympo
Illo uirgilium me tempore dulcis alebat
Parthenope studiis florentem ignobilis oti
Carmina qui lusi pastorum audaxq iuuenta
Tityre te patulae cecini sub tegmine fagi

FINIS. AMEN: DEO: GRATIAS

.P. V. M. GEORGICARVM LIB IIII EXPLICIT.

FLOKPHBNFS: DF PBRHB: SEKPSK

HPE. PXS. FFELICITER : &

Aeneas sacrificing; fragment of the frieze on the Altar of
Augustan Peace, Rome, 1st century BC. (Photo: Alinari)

P·VERGILII MARONIS
LIBER PRIMVS·

ILLE EGO
QVI QVON
DAM GRA
CILI MO
DVLATVS
AVENA
CARMEN; ET EGRESSVS
SILVIS VICINA COEGI
VT QVANVIS AVIDO PA
RERENT ARVA COLONO
GRATVM OPVS AGRICOLIS:
AT NVNC HORRENTIA MARTIS
ARMA VIRVMQ' CANO:TRO
IAE QVI PRIMVS AB ORIS
ITALIAM FATO PROFVGVS
LAVINIA VENIT

DVBIA · FORTVNA

The beginning of the *Aeneid* with a cameo of a battle scene, probably used here to represent the death of the Amazon Camilla; from a 15th-century Italian manuscript. (Add. MS 11355 f.79; British Library)

ABOVE: Dido and Aeneas riding out to hunt; detail from a 4th-century Roman mosaic pavement found at Low Ham, Somerset. (Somerset County Museum)

RIGHT: The storm that scattered Aeneas's fleet in the *Aeneid* 1; engraving by Pierre Lambart from a design by Francis Clein in Ogilby's English translation of Virgil which he published in 1654. (British Library)

BELOW: Papyrus fragment of a Roman writing exercise, 1st century AD, which repeats line 601 of the *Aeneid* 2. (Hawara Papyrus 24; University College, London)

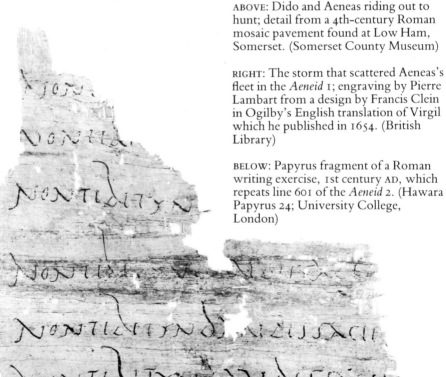

Suoemit, et duplices ten-
Talia voce refert: ô
Queis ante orâ Patrum
Contigit oppetere:
Honoratiss. Dom̃. Dõ
Equiti aurato, Comiti
Wentworth, Baroni
Woodhowse, Newmarch
    Tabula merito

dens ad sidera palmas,
terque quaterque beati
Troiâ sub mænibus altis

Guilielmo Wentworth
Straffordiæ, Vice Comiti
Wentworth de Wentworth
Overfley et Raby.
    votiva.

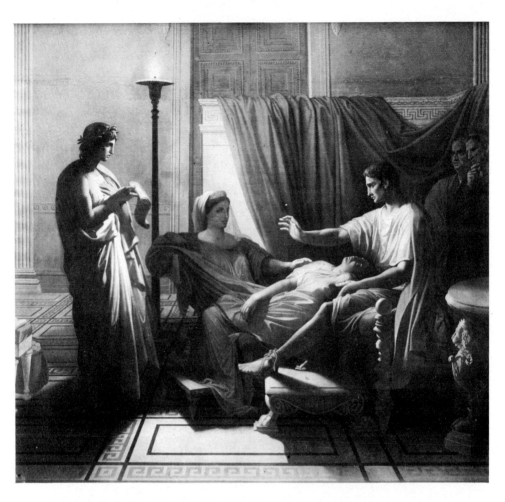

'Virgil reading the *Aeneid* to the Emperor Augustus', painting by
Ingres (1780–1867). (Toulouse Museum; photo: Mansell
Collection)

RIGHT: Italian 15th-century manuscript with a margin addition of
lines 567 to 588 of the *Aeneid* 2, in which Aeneas almost kills
Helen when he meets her in Troy. On Virgil's instructions, this
passage was deleted from the poem after his death. (Harley MS
2472 f. 19b; British Library)

h ic priamus quamquam in media iam morte tenetur
non tamen abstinuit nec uoci iraeque pepercit
a tibi pro scelere exclamat pro talibus ausis
di siqua est caelo pietas quae talia curet
persoluant grates dignas et praemia reddant
debita qui nati coram me cernere letum
fecisti et patrios foedasti sanguine uultus
at non ille satum quo te mentiris achilles
talis in hoste fuit priamo sed iura fidemque
supplicis erubuit corpusque exangue sepulcro
reddidit hectoreum meque in mea regna remisit
sic fatus senior telumque imbelle sine ictu
coniecit rauco quod protinus aere repulsum est
et summo clipei nequiquam umbone pependit
cui pyrrhus refers ergo haec et nuntius ibis
pelidae genitori illi mea tristia facta
degeneremque neoptolemum narrare memento
nunc morere hoc dicens altaria ad ipsa trementem
traxit et in multo lapsantem sanguine nati
implicuitque comam laeva dextraque coruscum
extulit ac lateri capulo tenus abdidit ensem
haec finis priami fatorum hic exitus illum
sorte tulit troiam incensam et prolapsa uidentem
pergama tot quondam populis terrisque superbum
regnatorem asiae iacet ingens litore truncus
auulsumque umeris caput et sine nomine corpus
bstupui subiit cari genitoris ymago
at metu primum seuus circumstetit horror
et regem aequievum crudeli vulnere uidi
uitam exalantem subiit et deserta creusa
et direpta domus et parui casus iuli
respicio et quae sit me circum copia lustro
deseruere omnes defessi et corpora saltu
ad terram misere aut ignibus aegra dedere
um mihi se non ante oculis tam clara uidendam
obtulit et pura per noctem in luce refulsit

...ulcisci patriam et sceleratas sumere penas
scilicet hic spartam incolumis patriasque mycenas
aspiciet partoque ibit regina triumpho
coniugium domumque patres natosque uidebit
iliadum turba et phrygiis comitata ministris
occiderit ferro priamus troia arserit igni
dardanium totiens sudarit sanguine litus
non ita namque etsi nullum memorabile nomen
feminea in poena est nec habet uictoria laudem

Exstinxisse nefas tamen et sumpsisse merentis
laudabor poenas animumque explesse iuvabit
ultricis flammae et cineres satiasse meorum
talia iactabam et furiata mente ferebar

Italian maiolica of the 15th century showing Dido enchanted by
Aeneas's son Ascanius. (British Museum)

RIGHT: A page from *Works of Virgil* published by Grüninger at
Strasbourg in 1502, with illustrations by Sebastian Brant. The
text is from the *Aeneid* 4, 77–84, but the illustration is of an
earlier passage where Venus and Juno plot to ensnare Dido
through Aeneas's son. (British Library)

Nunc eadem labente die conuiuia quęrit.

Iliacoſqʒ iterum demens audire labores

Expoſcit : pendetqʒ iterum narrantis ab ore.

Cur facũda parũ decoro inter verba cedit lingua ſilentio. D. Incipit affari. Precidebat cõtextũ ſpbo rũ:vt loquédi ſpacia pfer ret in longũ.C. Incipit af fari. Signũ maximi amo ris:cũ orõne integra non põt vti amãs:ſed vt puer interrũpit. Hanc rẽ mire oſtẽdit Florẽtⁱⁱ petrarcha in eo lyrico Benchio tabbía guardato: de menſogna:iuxta miã poſſa : & honorato aſſaſ ingra ta lingua non põgia inhaſ Renduro honore:ma factomi uergogna.Che quãto piu ſi tuo aſuto mi biſogna p do mãdare mercede allhor tiſtaı ſemp piu fredda:& ſe paro le ſa ſono impſecte & come dhuom che ſogna.Sed dicet aliquis:cum amor cautus:calliduſqʒ ſit:etiam eloquens erit:Vnde eſt ild:Diſertũ faciebat amor:Eſt quidẽ diſer tus amãs:ſed ſepe vel ſubito interuẽtu:vel vehemẽti aliı qua cogitatione ita conſternatur:vt omina e memoria

piebant:Eamqʒ coenam appellabant: . Deinde coeptum eſt:vt bis in die epularẽt.primamqʒ epulatiõe prãdiũ dixerunt.ſed de hoc raro meminerunt ſcriptores:niſi in vi ta laſſiurori:vt ſ:pe in Comitis videmus.
k   Illiacoſqʒ.D.conſumptis omnibus inuentionibus re dibat ad ea ꝗ prius erãt narrata:miſere illũ deunere cuꝑ piebant. l   Demens.S.quę ea quę nouerat cupꝛbat au dire.   m   Pendet narrantis ab ore.S.vt cũ intuere tur.et hoc loco per omnia amantis affectus exprimitur. ı CRI.Pendet ab ore.Nã amantes omnia quę ab amato dicuntur:qualiacunqʒ ſunt admirantur.

excidant:ſubitoqʒ mute ſcant.   i   Labẽte die. .S quia in vſu nõ erãt pran dia:vt Iuuenal. Exul ꝛb octaua marius bibit. C. Labente die.Ex more ro mano:qui ſeſin die & id pⁱ ſolis occaſum cibũ ca

 ꝙn Obſcura lũa.S.i. nox: Nã nihil tã cõtrariũ eſt lune q̃ obſcuritas. o   Sola.S.ſineeo quem amabat. Nã regina ſola eſſe nõ poterat . Eſt autẽ Plautiꝗ inducit amatoꝛ rẽ:inter mⁱ:os poſitũ diꝰ centẽ cp ſolus ſit. p   Mœret.S.p dyphthõ gon eſt triſtis:aliter ſigni

 ꝙ poſt vbi digreſſi:lumẽqʒ obſcura viciſſim:

Luna premit:ſuadẽtqʒ cadẽtia ſydera ſomnos.

Sola domo mœret vacua:ſtratiſqʒ relictis

Incubat:illum abſens abſẽte auditqʒ videtqʒ:

Aut gremio Aſcaniũ genitoris imagine capta

ficat militat:vt acre mos rẽt:paruo. Sane mœreoꝛ aliud eſt. q   Abſens ab ſentẽ.S.Teren.Pñs. pſen tẽ:eripi abduci ab ocuſ. D. Illũ abſens . tm falleꝛ baſ amãtis anım²: vt ab ſentẽ videri & audire ſiꝰ bi viderẽ.   r   Imagine cap.S.amãtis ſiſitudine: ſ   Si fallere poſ.a. C.ꝗ̃ſ

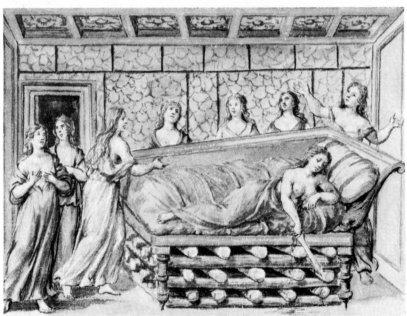

Illustrations to *Aeneid* 4. (Top) Dido commits suicide, while in the background the Trojans land in Carthage, Aeneas kills a stag, and Dido and Aeneas ride out to hunt, passing the cave where they shelter from the storm; late 15th-century manuscript by Bartolomeo Sanvito. (Kings MS 24 f. 101b; British Library) (Above) Dido sets fire to her funeral pyre; copied by Pietro Santi Bartoli in 1677 from the fragmentary 4th-century manuscript 'Schedae Vaticanae'. (Lansdowne MS 834 f. 51; British Library)

[The pale cheekt gromor w[ith] ther unguiltie bloud]
So Dido wrapt away w[ith] ... passion
And fervent love that cannot be withstood
Went raging in soe strange a fashion
    Unto the walles as yet not finished.
    For ... she was soe much enamored.

As that shee showd him all her ... treasure
Faine would she speake, but feares by shame was staide
All her desire was but to yeild him pleasure
Now shee besought, desird, beseecht, and praid
    That whilst her tender armes his neck enronde
    Ever more she ... his woefull tale was tolld.

But when the glittering Moone made manifest
Black night approach, and twinckling starrs disclose
Ther lesser lights. The Quene w[ith] griefe opprest
Upon a bed her weary Limmes repose
    On w[hom] t Æneas oft had dallyed
    Ascanius on her knee she dandeled.

In whose swete face was lively represented
His fathers eye and gracefull modestie
In looking on she could not rest contented
... ... her lustfull love could satisfie.
    And now no ... were traind nor armes prepard,
    No Bulwarks nor strong fortresses were reard

Translation of the *Aeneid* 4 in stanza form by Sir John
Haryngton, done in the 1580s when it was thought more proper
to translate Virgil in stanzas than in couplets used earlier. (Add.
MS 60283 f. 3; British Library)

River god appearing to Aeneas in a dream; illustration to the
Aeneid 8 by Francis Clein for Ogilby's *Works of Virgil*, published
in English 1654 and in Latin 1658. (British Museum)

RIGHT: The beginning of the *Aeneid*, from a late 15th-century
Italian manuscript. Despite the splendour of its elaborate border,
filled with flowers, animals and putti, and its beautiful script,
numerous reader's notes have been added between the lines.
(Burney MS 270 f. 1; British Library)

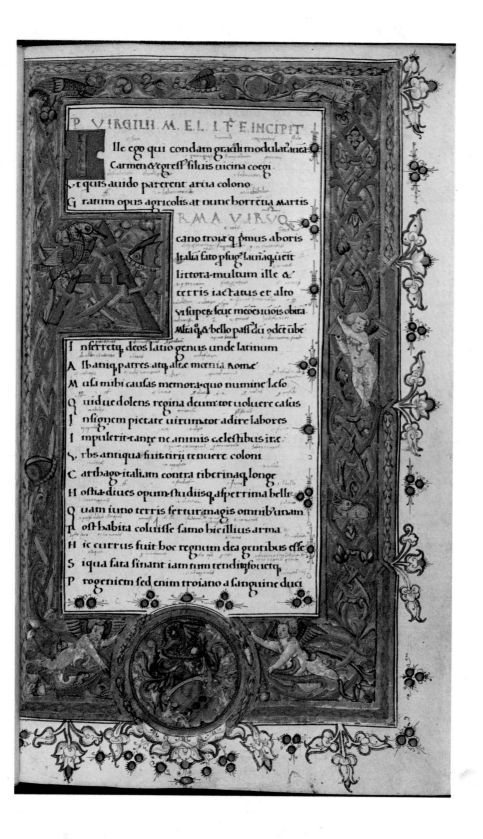

P. VIRGILII. M. E. L. I. F E INCIPIT

Ille ego qui condam gracili modulatus auena
Carmen & egress siluis uicina coegi.
Ut quis auido parerent artia colono
Gratum opus agricolis at nunc horrentia martis

RMA VIRVO
cano troie q pmus aboris
Italia fato pfug' lauiaq.uenit
littora·multum ille &
terris iactatus et alto
ui supei seue meces iuois obira
alta q.& bello passi du odet ube
Inferretq. deos latio·genus unde latinum
Albaniq.patres atq.alte menia Rome·
Musa mihi causas memora·quo numine leso
Quidue dolens regina deum·tot uoluere casus
Insignem pietate uirum·tot adire labores
Impulerit·tante ne animis celestibus ire·
Urbs antiqua fuit·tirii tenuere coloni
Carthago·italiam contra tiberinaq.longe
Hostia·diues opum·studiisq.asperrima belli
Quam iuno terris fertur·magis omnib'unam
Post habita coluisse samo·hic illius arma
Hic currus fuit·hoc regnum dea gentibus esse
Siqua fata sinant·iam tum tenditq.fouetq.
Progeniem sed enim troiano a sanguine duci

Membra sequebantur. nec longo deinde moranti
Tempore contactos artus sacer ignis edebat.
P·OVIDII IN·IIII·GEORGICON VIRGILII·
ROTINVS aerii mellis redolentia regna
Hyblæasq́; apes. aluoꝛ; & cærea tecta.
Quiq́; alibi flores. examina quæq́; legenda
Indicat: humentisq́; fauos cælestia dona.

P·VIR·MARONIS GE
ORGICON LIBER·IV·
AD MECAENATEM·

ROTINVS
AERII MEL
LIS CAELE
STIA DNA

PART II

Virgil through the Ages

T. S. PATTIE

LEFT: The opening page of the *Georgics* 4, showing its subject of bees and bee-keeping; from a late 15th-century manuscript written and illuminated by Bartolomeo Sanvito. (Kings MS 24 f.47b; British Library)

5

THE TRADITION OF THE TEXT

As many as six hundred manuscripts of Virgil's works may have survived, more than for any other classical author unless, as is claimed, there are even more of the dramatist Terence. Moreover, these include three more or less complete manuscripts which date from as early as the fourth and fifth centuries. This excellent manuscript tradition is not altogether surprising given Virgil's popularity and status. In his own lifetime his reputation guaranteed the accurate and widespread copying of his work, and after his death in 19 BC his poems became classics throughout the Roman Empire. The Emperor Hadrian, who ruled from AD 117 to 138, is said to have consulted Virgil's poems as a sort of oracle and if so, they were being treated as a sacred text within a century and a half of the poet's death.

At that time literary works were copied on papyrus in rolls, which were held horizontally, not vertically like today's scrolls. There is a limit to how much writing can conveniently be held on one roll and Virgil's poems would be copied in parts: one roll might hold a single book of the *Aeneid* in a handsomely written, well-spaced format. The papyrus roll was thought the proper medium for literary works and anything else was looked down on as 'not a proper book'; parchment, made from animal skin, which is supposed to have been invented in the third or second century BC, was considered an inferior medium and was used for notebooks or school exercises.

Egypt was the classical world's only producer of papyrus, made from the pith of the papyrus reed which used to grow extensively in Egypt and still grows wild today in millions of acres in Uganda. Seventeen fragments of Virgil dating from the early centuries and written on papyrus or parchment have been found in Egypt and one in Palestine from a Roman colony. Only three of them are earlier than the three major Virgil manuscripts that survive from the fourth and fifth centuries, and the two earliest are mere writing exercises, of which the 'Hawara Virgil' in University College, London, dates from the first century AD. The lines of poetry used on this papyrus fragment are probably the ancient equivalent of our typing practice line, 'The quick brown fox jumps over the lazy dog.' The third is a fragment of a parchment roll containing fifteen lines from the fifth *Eclogue*, although why a parchment roll should have been used for a literary work remains a puzzle. Perhaps it follows Jewish traditions, like the Dead Sea Scrolls. Most of the other fragments seem to be school books and none of them is of particular value, partly because they come from the provinces, partly because they are mainly school exercises, several with Greek literal translations, and above all because of the other very early and reliable copies of Virgil's text.

There were dramatic developments in the technology of book production in the early Christian centuries, and some believe that the Christians were responsible for these changes. It is certain that they did not feel bound by tradition, for they did not continue to use the papyrus roll, like the classical Greeks and Romans, nor the parchment roll, like the Jews. To write the books of the Bible, the Christians more and more used the codex – the paged book as we know it – first on papyrus and then on parchment. Whether the Christians sponsored the change or merely adopted it, the reign of Constantine the Great in the fourth century saw both the triumph of Christianity in the Roman Empire and a revolution in book production which made it possible for the first time to make books big enough to hold all of Virgil's poems in one volume, or to hold in one volume the whole Bible, which is even bigger.

So we need not be surprised not to have any complete or nearly complete manuscript of Virgil before the fourth century. And even this interval of over four hundred years between the author's own manuscript and the first surviving copy is less than for any other classical author. For many the interval is a thousand years, in some cases more – we know Catullus, Virgil's contemporary, through a single thirteenth-century manuscript, which was subsequently lost. Even from a later period, there are only a few writers whose works survive in manuscripts that are nearly contemporary with the author. One of them is the Venerable Bede (673–735), for whom we have two manuscripts which were written within twenty years of his death. Only the Greek Bible has a better early manuscript tradition than Virgil: three complete or nearly complete manuscripts of the fourth and fifth centuries. (Two of them are in the British Library.)

Altogether eight manuscripts of Virgil, some of them with pictures, survive from the fourth and fifth centuries. Five are mere fragments but the other three alone are sufficient to establish Virgil's text. These are the fifth-century Mediceus (M), once owned by the Medici family and now in the Laurentian Library in Florence, the fourth- or fifth-century Palatinus (P) in the Vatican Library, and the fifth-century Romanus (R), also in the Vatican Library. The Mediceus has lost the first 467 lines out of the 830 lines of the *Eclogues*, the Palatinus has lost about a tenth of the whole of Virgil's poems, and the Romanus about a fifth. All told, there is at least one ancient witness for all of Virgil's work, at least two for ninety-seven per cent of it, and three or more for seventy-seven per cent.

Virgil through the Ages

Hardly any Virgil manuscripts have come down to us from the confused and turbulent sixth to eighth centuries but with the return of political stability under Charlemagne (742–814), there was a revival of learning, and at least twelve Virgil manuscripts survive from the ninth century. These are a valuable, but not indispensable, support to the earliest manuscripts. Of the twelve, four are now in Paris and five in Berne.

The earliest Virgils in the British Library are two tenth-century fragments: two leaves of Harley MS 3072, containing *Eclogues* 2. 32 to 3. 74, and fifteen leaves in Harley MS 2772, containing various portions of Books 7 to 11 of the *Aeneid*. Of the later manuscripts, about three-quarters – sixty-one to be precise – date from the fifteenth century, with four from the fourteenth, ten from the thirteenth, one from the twelfth and one, another fragment, from the eleventh century. Most of them were written in Italy.

The older the manuscript, the better its text is a useful rule of thumb, but is not always true, for some of our fifteenth-century manuscripts seem to be better than some of our thirteenth-century ones. If we can show that one manuscript is copied from another, we need spend no more time on the copy. Unfortunately, we cannot always be sure that one manuscript was copied directly and exclusively from another. The British Library can illustrate a rare chain of three manuscripts (A copied from B, B copied from C) of a collection, formed about 1500, of polemical tracts arguing that kings should keep their hands off church lands. But more often the position is uncertain, or as with Catullus, all the surviving manuscripts may be copies of a single manuscript.

With Virgil the case is particularly complicated not only because so many manuscripts have survived but also because these have been extensively corrected from each other. This makes it difficult to trace the family tree and to know whether a good text is the result of accurate copying or intelligent editing.

The Tradition of the Text

Although we already have a very early and reliable text for Virgil and do not need to rely on later manuscripts, these are always interesting in showing us how Virgil was studied and read at a particular time and place. A good text may be used as a standard by which to judge the spelling and competence of the others, and manuscripts searched for clues to changes in the sounds and grammar of their vernacular, for example, Italian scribes write 'x' for 's' and 'z' for 'x'.

Some of the manuscripts may also provide interesting sidelights on their owners' tastes. Parchment can be re-used by scraping off the original writing, and among the manuscripts treated in this way is one of the five early fragments already mentioned, which is now in Verona. Virgil's text was scraped off in the seventh century and Part II of Pope Gregory's *Moral Sayings on Job* written over it, although the underwriting can still be read in places. Similarly in the British Library's Additional MS 16166, written in England in the fourteenth century, an owner lost interest in Virgil and began to scrape several pages clean in order to write medical recipes. Sometimes it worked the other way: in the fourteenth century a land register at Castel Franco in Italy was scraped clean and cut into leaves for the scribe Andrea Bartholomeo, or Bartholomeo Andrea, to write the *Aeneid* (now Additional MS 23897).

One criterion by which the surviving Virgil manuscripts can be classified is to count the number of lines supplemented in the *Aeneid*. When Virgil died, he had still to do the final polishing up of his great epic and about fifty lines were left uncompleted. The temptation to supplement these lines proved too strong for many scribes and the 'worst' manuscripts in the British Library collection have as many as eleven lines supplemented, for example, the fifteenth-century Additional MS 11955 and Harley MS 3518. The 'best' have only one supplemented line, and in this class are Additional MS 11355 and Harley MS 5261, both de luxe fifteenth-century manuscripts.

The thirteenth-century Harley MS 2668 also has only one supplemented line, but as it contains only one third of the *Aeneid* it could belong to the average class, which has three to five lines supplemented.

Three lines are by far the most commonly supplemented, of which the first is line 340 in Book 3: *Quem tibi iam Troia*... (literally, 'Whom to you with Troy now...'). It occurs in the passage where Aeneas and his companions have visited Andromache, now residing in the kingdom of Pyrrhus. Andromache is breathless for news: 'What of the boy Ascanius? Is he still alive? Whom to you with Troy now...'. The line remains incomplete in the three earliest surviving manuscripts but in all but eight of the British Library manuscripts the line has been completed, to make it mean '(Ascanius) whom Creusa bore you while Troy was burning/besieged/still flourishing' – and there are a number of other variations. No doubt 'besieged' and 'still flourishing' were corrections designed to counter the objection that Ascanius must have been born at least some months before Troy was burnt. The very variety of readings tells against the genuineness of the supplements and helps confirm that the line was left incomplete in Virgil's original text.

The second of these supplements, line 661 in Book 3, comes when Aeneas and his companions have just rescued Achaemenides, who had been left behind in Sicily by Odysseus, and they have all seen the Cyclops, blind and using a stick to guide him. To the line, he has his sheep for 'his only pleasure and the consolation for his misfortune' has been added the words *de collo fistula pendet* – 'his pipe (his consolation in misfortune) hangs from his neck'. This supplement is found in nine of the twelve ninth-century manuscripts used by R.A.B. Mynors in his standard Oxford edition of Virgil, and in the corrections, perhaps also of the ninth century, to one of the three chief manuscripts, as well as in all the British Library manuscripts with the solitary exception of Additional MS 11355.

In the third of these commonly supplemented lines, Virgil is describing the ceremony of the 'Game of Troy', which he likens to the intricate passages of the Labyrinth. The Trojan boys perform mock battles like swimming dolphins 'who cut the Carpathian and Libyan seas'. The supplement 'and play among the waves' makes good sense and would be unexceptionable except that only the Romanus of the ancient manuscripts and only two of the twelve ninth-century manuscripts include it. All the British Library manuscripts have it except four: Additional MS 21910, Arundel MS 193, Burney MS 270 and Harley MS 5261. Burney MS 270 makes a surprising appearance here since it has no less than eight lines supplemented, placing it in the second worst class on this criterion.

Other lines of the *Aeneid* have come down to us only because they are preserved by Servius, the fourth-century scholar whose commentary is an invaluable source of information about Virgil's poems. Virgil was not satisfied with the passage in Book 2, lines 567–588, where Aeneas, raging through the burning city of Troy, meets Helen cowering on the steps of the temple of Vesta. In his fury he is about to kill the woman who has brought destruction to his beloved Troy, when at the critical moment he sees in a vision his mother Venus, who tells him to leave Helen for the gods to deal with and to find his father, wife, and son whose lives are in great danger. Perhaps Virgil felt that the picture of Helen skulking in fear was inconsistent with her active collaboration with the Greeks, which is narrated by Deiphobus in the Underworld (Book 6. 511–530), but whatever the reason Virgil's executors, Varius and Tucca, were evidently instructed to delete the passage.

Both the Mediceus and the Palatinus (the Romanus has a

gap at this point) omit the lines, as do most of the ninth-century manuscripts, and only seven out of fifty-four of the British Library manuscripts have the passage in as part of the text. Another includes it but marked as doubtful or spurious; two more omit it from the body of the text but add it in the margin; and a third includes it in an appendix at the end of the manuscript. The manuscripts with the passage in have varying numbers of supplemented half-lines so by that criterion there are 'good', 'bad', and 'average' manuscripts among them. Did they all get the Helen episode from Servius independently, or do they all go back to a single source, or to a few sources? We just do not know.

Scholars have tried for five hundred years, and especially for the last 150 years, to restore exactly what Virgil himself wrote. Although the 'ideal text' is bound to be to some extent hypothetical, we confidently call all variations from it 'errors'. In some cases these variations are such manifest nonsense that there is no question but that they are genuine mistakes. In other cases, it is a matter of judgement and comparison with other expressions of the poet. In general, manuscripts that agree in a correct text cannot be assumed to be related to each other, but those that consistently agree in errors are likely to have some relationship.

One manuscript that contains many errors is the British Library's Burney MS 270, which has already been classed as 'bad' in that it adds supplements to eight of the half-lines in the *Aeneid*. The calligraphy is beautiful but the scribe reveals himself as only too human. He left out four lines in Book 9 which had to be added in the margin and he sometimes tried to conceal corrections by putting the correct word in the margin and calling it a 'variant reading'. For example, the god of harbours, Portunus, appears in the text as 'portundus' with 'portunus' as an alternative reading in the margin. Instead of 'butroti' (of Buthrotum) he wrote 'iditroti', and instead of

'Xanthum' (Xanthus – the city near Troy) he wrote 'sanctum' (holy) and later corrected it to 'zantum'. Was he writing from dictation or reading aloud to himself so that he heard the sound but missed the sense?

Sometimes we can see how this scribe made his mistakes. 'Signum' (sign) is written for 'sic nam' (for thus) in the line after 'signum' has appeared and, besides, 'c' and 'g' are easily confused in some scripts. At one place where a line is repeated and then deleted, we can see from the slightly different colour of the ink that the repeat was made after the scribe had broken off from his work and begun again later with a freshly mixed supply of ink. He wrote 'amnis' (river) instead of 'annis' (from our years), probably because in the manuscript he was copying the word appeared as 'añis' and the bar could stand for either 'm' or 'n'. Likewise when he wrote 'umbra' (shadow) instead of 'verba' (words), he had probably wrongly expanded what was written as 'v'ba'. In another place, his eye seems to have jumped from the word 'Italiam' in *Aeneid* 1. 553 to the same word in the following line, so that Ilioneus, leader of the larger part of Aeneas's fleet, separated from Aeneas in a storm, asks Dido for permission to refit his ships, 'if it is given us to seek Italy and Latium joyfully', rather than 'if it is given us to recover our king and companions and make for Italy, so that we may seek Italy and Latium joyfully'.

A later scribe added a series of alternative readings to the text, with the result that the manuscript has lost much of its original beauty and elegance, but the errors in Burney MS 270 illustrate many of the kinds of mistakes that scribes made in copying, similar examples of which could be found in any newspaper today.

Virgil was one of the most frequently printed authors once printing was introduced to Europe – the British Library alone has nearly a hundred different editions up to 1500 – and they all used what is often called the 'vulgate text', that is, the text of most of the later manuscripts. This includes the line, *Eclogues* 4. 62, 'the baby on whom his parents have not smiled will not be thought worthy of a god's table or a goddess's bed'. Today we are certain because of clues in the quotation of Virgil by another Roman writer, Quintilian, that what Virgil actually wrote was 'the baby who has not smiled at his parents will not be thought worthy of a god's table or a goddess's bed'. This after all was the child who was to bring back the Golden Age, and must be as remarkable as Hercules who strangled two snakes while still a few days old.

Again, at *Eclogue* 7. 48, the early printed editions, and some more recent ones, as well as all the British Library manuscripts, have 'the buds are swelling in the *joyful* vine shoots', but the modern reading prefers 'the *pliant* vine shoots'. And at *Eclogue* 8. 107 all the manuscripts and all the first printed editions have 'Hylas [the shepherd's dog] is barking at the threshold'. Since Hylas was a handsome youth beloved of Hercules, this does not make good sense, and in the edition of 1500/1501 the scholar Jodocus Badius Ascensius made the correct conjecture that 'Hylas' should read 'Hylax', or 'Barker', a most suitable name for a dog.

Aside from the reading of the text, these early printed books are often beautiful in themselves. They set out to imitate manuscripts as closely as possible, using type which was cut to resemble contemporary handwriting, and using layouts of the page which were identical to those in contemporary manuscripts. Parchment rather than paper continued to be used for de luxe books for some time after the introduction of printing, and in some particularly luxurious books illustrations were painted in by hand after the book was printed; for this purpose vellum gave a more satisfactory surface than paper. One example is the Virgil printed on vellum by Aldus Manutius of Venice in 1501, with beautiful hand-painted illustrations, which was once in the library of the Gonzaga family in Mantua (now British Library C.19.f.7) and may have been read by Isabella d'Este.

For all the Virgil manuscripts that have come down to us, scholars have concentrated on a limited number of venerable ones, rightly considering the rest as unnecessary for the establishment of the poet's text. The majority of the manuscripts are, however, useful as evidence of where and when Virgil's poems were read at various ages between his time and our own, and their relationships to each other and to the principal manuscripts remain to be elucidated. As for what Virgil actually wrote, we now have enough close, even microscopic, studies of his habits of composition and style of language to answer the question, 'Would he have said this in this way?'. In general over the last hundred years there have been great improvements in the reliability of Latin texts, and in the particular case of Virgil we can feel confident that two thousand years later the text we have is very close to what the poet himself wrote.

6

THE POPULAR TRADITIONS

Virgil's greatness as a poet was recognized during his lifetime not only by his fellow-poets but by the whole Roman people. Almost immediately his works were read and studied in schools throughout the Empire, and the *Aeneid* with its appeal to patriotism and duty was particularly valued. Some of his verses were scribbled, probably by schoolboys, on the walls of Pompeii, certainly before AD 79 when Pompeii was destroyed and possibly decades earlier. His poetry was discussed and read aloud in fashionable Roman circles, and it was familiar at all levels of society. It was frequently recited in theatres to great popular acclaim, and the *Aeneid* and in particular the moving story of Dido were part of the popular imagination.

All the signs that Virgil would enjoy lasting fame were there from very early on, and within less than two centuries of his death his work had become an object of almost superstitious veneration. It became a classic and, like the Bible, it was considered to have the mysterious powers of an oracle. Both Christians and pagans when in doubt would open Virgil at random to see what message it might have for them. According to the *Historia Augusta*, written in late antiquity, Hadrian and Alexander Severus, both future emperors of Rome, consulted this 'oracle', known as the *sortes Vergilianae*, to find what the future had in store for them. Hadrian, worried whether his uncle, the Emperor Trajan, would adopt him as his heir, is

reported to have opened Virgil to find these words from the
Aeneid:

> *Quis procul ille autem ramis insignis olivae*
> *sacra ferens? nosco crinis incanaque menta*
> *regis Romani, primam qui legibus urbem*
> *fundabit, Curibus parvis et paupere terra*
> *missus in imperium magnum.*
>
> (6. 808–812)

> But what's the man, who from afar appears
> His head with olive crowned, his hand a censer bears?
> His hoary beard and holy vestments bring
> His lost idea back: I know the Roman king.
> He shall to peaceful Rome new laws ordain,
> Called from his mean abode, a sceptre to sustain.
>
> (tr. Dryden)

The passage, with its mention of *magnum imperium* which
Dryden translates as 'sceptre', gave Hadrian just the reassurance
he needed for his hopes of attaining the imperial throne.

The Christians found a particularly prophetic message in
Virgil's fourth *Eclogue*, the famous 'Messianic Eclogue' of
about 41/40 BC, in which Virgil celebrates the birth of a son
who will introduce a glorious and peaceful future. Despite the
passage's ambiguities, it was naturally taken as a prediction of
the birth of Christ and Virgil was claimed as 'a Christian
without Christ'. The fourth-century Christian father and
classical scholar, St Jerome, quotes the lines (*Eclogue* 4. 6–7) in a
letter to St Paulinus, Bishop of Nola in Italy, in which he
discusses the study of the scriptures:

> *Iam redit et Virgo, redeunt Saturnia regna*
> *Iam nova progenies caelo demittitur alto.*

Now the Maid has come again, Saturn's Kingdom has
returned and the new-born son is sent down from the
skies.

Jerome's letter quoting Virgil was prefaced to nearly all Latin
Vulgate Bibles from the ninth century. The British Library
alone has at least one hundred Vulgates with this preface,
including the huge and splendid Moutier-Grandval Bible
(Additional MS 10546), which was written at Tours in about
830 in a beautiful Carolingian minuscule.

The Christian fathers frequently quoted Virgil to support
their moral arguments. For example, Jerome used the story of
Dido to warn widows of the consequences of marrying again.
The lines he quotes on more than one occasion are *Aeneid* 4. 32–
34 and 548–552. In the first passage Dido's sister urges her to
break her vow of eternal faithfulness to her dead husband
Sychaeus:

> *solane perpetua maerens carpere iuventa*
> *nec dulcis natos Veneris nec praemia noris?*
> *id cinerem aut manis credis curare sepultos?*

> Will you to grief your blooming years bequeath,
> Condemned to waste in woes your lonely life,
> Without the joys of mother, or of wife?
> Think you these tears, this pompous train of woe,
> Are known or valued by the ghosts below?   (tr. Dryden)

In the second passage Dido in despair laments the dreadful
consequences of her lapse from chastity:

> *tu lacrimis euicta meis, tu prima furentem*
> *his, germana, malis oneras atque obicis hosti.*
> *non licuit thalami expertem sine crimine vitam*

degere more ferae, talis nec tangere curas;
non servata fides cineri promissa Sychaeo.

Your pity, sister, first seduced my mind,
Or seconded too well what I designed.
These dear-bought pleasures had I never known,
Had I continued free, and still my own –
Avoiding love, I had not found despair,
But shared with savage beasts the common air.
Like them, a lonely life I might have led,
Not mourned the living, nor disturbed the dead.

(tr. Dryden)

Many classical authors besides Virgil were used in this way. A much more curious development, however, was the Cento, in which lines and parts of lines of the great poets were re-combined to form new poems, often with startling results. The Latin poet Ausonius (c.310–393/4) composed a poem called 'Wedding Cento', made up of lines of Virgil, to which he added a preface apologizing for the frivolity of his 'little poem which has been neither forged by toil nor finished with the file'. A lady called Proba Falconia, wife of the late fourth-century proconsul Adelfius, made a Cento of Virgil about the creation of the world and the life of Christ. St Gregory of Nazianzos (c.328–390) made a Cento of Euripides's *Bacchae* entitled 'Christ's Agony'.

The vogue for composing Centos marked a stage in the process of accommodating pagan literature to Christian purposes and, however absurd, it shows a great familiarity with Virgil's works. Proba in her Cento puts the words of Venus to Cupid when she plots to ensnare Dido (*Aeneid* 1.664) in the mouth of God the Father speaking of Christ at his baptism:

Nate meae vires, mea magna potentia solus.

Virgil through the Ages

My son, you alone are my strength, my great power.

In another, Virgil's description of Anchises when he says that he will never leave his native Troy (*Aeneid* 2. 650) is applied to Christ nailed to the Cross:

Talia perstabat memorans, fixusque manebat

He stood there saying these words, and remained without
  moving.

Jerome in his letter to Paulinus is, not surprisingly, scornful of the whole business, describing the Cento as 'puerile'. Nevertheless Renaissance poetasters revived the practice of plundering the treasures of Virgil to compose poems like the 'Aeneis sacra' or the 'Virgilius evangelizans' or the 'Virgilian Cento against Women' (written by Lelio Capilupi, the Renaissance scholar who is said to have owned Harley MS 2744).

The process of assimilating classical authors into Christianity was not achieved without opposition, for some Christians unsympathetic to literature made violent denunciations of the pagan gods in classical texts. Even Jerome, an ardent lover of literature, had a dream in which he saw himself before the judgement seat of God and heard a voice accusing him of being no Christian, but a Ciceronian; after this he withdrew to the desert to flee the blandishments of classical literature. But classical works could not be ignored, even if they were pagan, and with Virgil as the greatest Latin poet and Latin as the language of the Church, Virgil's poems continued to form the chief textbook in the schools of grammar, to be widely used as a quarry for quotations, and to be admired by scholars and general public alike. Virgil's reputation as a fount of wisdom and his supposed Messianic prophecy ensured his fame, and gave him almost the status of a Christian saint.

The Popular Traditions

Dante in his *Divina Commedia* has Virgil guide him through the Inferno and Purgatory as far as the Earthly Paradise, and only because Virgil was born too soon to become a Christian does he then leave Dante to be guided by Beatrice through Paradise. It is also because of Virgil's prophecy of Christ's birth that, according to legend, the first-century Latin poet Statius (much more admired in the Middle Ages than now) was led to repent and become a Christian, and Statius too is included in the *Divina Commedia* as the companion of Dante and Virgil through part of Purgatory.

Dante's admiration of Virgil was not always shared by other Christians of the early Middle Ages. We hear frequent denunciations of the devils in the shapes of Virgil and Ovid who led simple souls astray. Herbert, Bishop of Norwich, speaking in the twelfth century, objected to monks reading Ovid's lies and Virgil's inventions, for 'it is improper for the same mouth to recite Ovid and to preach Christ' – a phrase which also reminds us that most people used to read aloud even to themselves. We even hear of people being executed for saying that the classical poets were unimpeachable guides to conduct. Perhaps something more sinister was involved: the pagan gods may have been invoked in magic spells to satisfy guilty lust, and maybe the accusations of carnal intercourse with the Devil made in the witchcraft trials of the seventeenth century were a reflection of what was suspected in an earlier age.

Certainly in the Middle Ages Virgil acquired an extraordinary reputation in folk mythology as a magician. Virgil had followed in his eighth *Eclogue* the Hellenistic tradition of writing short poems about magic and spells and, like Theocritus, he wrote about a girl trying to compel her faithless lover to come back to her. Virgil, however, clearly did not share the common belief in magic for he distanced the magic practices described in the poem by putting them in the mouth of one of the singers. Nevertheless, this in combination with the *sortes Vergilianae* would probably have given sufficient grounds for readers to attribute magic powers to Virgil. This reputation seems to have first been recorded in the twelfth century but it may have existed in popular legend for many years before that. Many of these stories are associated with Naples, the city where with nearby Nola Virgil spent most of his adult life.

The Englishman Gervase of Tilbury, who spent much of his life in court circles in Italy and France, records Virgil's supposed magical practices around the Naples area in his *Otia Imperialia* or *Recreations of an Emperor*, dedicated to the Holy Roman Emperor Otto IV in 1212, a time when much of Italy had been brought under the political control of the great mediaeval empire of the Germans. The stories about Virgil are included in the part of Gervase's book entitled 'The Marvels of the World' – 'those things marvellous which we do not understand even though they be natural. . . . Let no one doubt the veracity of what I record.' Among the marvellous things he recorded are a brass fly which, as long as it remained undamaged and in its proper place on one of Naples' fortified gates, preserved all Campania from flies, and a piece of meat which Virgil had placed in an abattoir and which kept all the meat there fresh.

Gervase also records a story about the two marble faces, one on each side of the city gate of Nola, the proof of which he reports to have seen with his own eyes. The story as he tells it, with much circumstantial detail, is that in 1190 he was in Salerno when he met an English friend with whom he decided to travel. After an unsuccessful attempt to arrange a ferry at an acceptable price, they travelled to Nola where they were entertained by Giovanni Pinatelli, the archdeacon of Naples. While a feast was being prepared for them, they went out and this time successfully arranged a ferry for a certain day. On their return they talked of the surprising ease with which they had accomplished their mission. 'Ho', said the archdeacon, 'which city gate did you come in by?... Please tell me exactly which part of the entrance you used, the right or the left?' They answered, 'Although we came to this gate and were about to go in on the left, suddenly an ass loaded with wood got in the way, and we were forced to turn to the right.' To this, the archdeacon replied: 'I want you to see what great marvels Virgil has worked in this city. Let's go to the place, and I'll show you what Virgil has left in that gate as a memorial on earth.' What he showed them was a smiling marble face in the wall on the right and a scowling marble face on the left. He explained: 'Whoever enters the city by the right always has a happy outcome of his endeavours; whoever turns to the left always fails and is cheated of all his desires. You turned to the right because the ass got in the way, and look how quickly and successfully you arranged your journey.' And Gervase finishes his chapter, 'We have mentioned this in admiration of Virgil's magic arts, and not to doubt God's providence.'

Similar tales are told by Conrad von Querfurt, Chancellor of the Emperor Henry VI and viceregent in Naples and Sicily. He tells how the people of Naples regarded Virgil as the special protector of the city, almost its patron saint, and that he had left with them an 'image' of the city in a glass bottle enclosed in an iron box which would protect them from attacks. The image – no doubt a statue of a woman with turreted headgear like the traditional Hellenistic city-personifications – worked its powers to save Naples from invasion in the 1130s and again from Emperor Henry VI's assault in 1191, but it did not avail against the Emperor's second expedition of 1194. Conrad attributes this failure to a crack in the bottle, but since he himself was in command of the besieging force, he may not have been entirely serious.

Earlier and independently from Gervase and Conrad, John of Salisbury, Bishop of Chartres (d.1180), makes sceptical mention of Virgil's magical powers. In his *Polycraticus*, finished in 1159, an encyclopaedia of miscellanies which started out as a treatise on the principles of government, he tells the story of Virgil's magic fly (*Polycraticus* 1.4; Royal MS 13 D.iv, f.9). According to this, Virgil finds Marcellus, nephew of Emperor Augustus, enthusiastically destroying the bird population (John of Salisbury was clearly unsympathetic to blood sports) and offers him the choice of a magic bird to capture birds, or a magic fly to exterminate flies. Marcellus discusses the matter with his uncle and decides on the fly, thereby ridding Naples of a terrible plague of flies. John thus also makes his moral point: public good outweighs private pleasure.

Elsewhere he records, with scorn and disgust, that he met in Apulia a certain Ludovicus (*Polycraticus* 2.23; Royal MS 13 D.iv. ff.28b—29) who was wasting much toil, sweat, hunger and sleepless nights in a vain quest to find Virgil's bones and take them back to Gaul. He would have done better, says John, to look for Virgil's good sense. Ludovicus, however, was offering a thousand aurei to anyone who would help him achieve his aim; met by refusal, he offered double, and finally broke into a shameless bray and made a gesture with his fingers to the bystanders to show their foolishness in not taking so much money for nothing.

The theologian and scientist, Alexander Neckham, who died in 1216, also tells of the magical creations of Virgil (Royal MSS 12 F.xiv, f.53b; 12 G.xi, ff.88–88b). These include the story of the golden leech which was thrown down a well and rid Naples of a plague of leeches; when many years later the well was cleared out, hordes of leeches immediately re-infested the city and only after the golden leech had been thrown back into the well did the hordes vanish. He also gives the story of the magic abattoir but in his version the meat is kept fresh for fifty years rather than indefinitely, as Gervase had reported. A new legend that Neckham introduces is that Virgil built a noble palace with wooden statues corresponding to all the regions of the Roman Empire. Each statue holds a bell in its hand and whenever some region plots against the Empire, the tell-tale statue begins to ring its bell and a bronze knight on the roof of the palace, spear in hand, points in the direction of the trouble. The poet, when asked how long this noble building would be preserved by the gods, replied: 'It will stand until a virgin gives birth.' Those who heard him applauded, saying 'It will stand for ever', but at the birth of the Saviour, the house is said to have suddenly crumbled into ruins.

From such stories of Virgil as the foreteller of Christ's coming, protector of Naples and universal benefactor, there developed all sorts of absurd and earthy tales attached to the disreputable magician known as Virgil. Several early printed books have traditional collections of these, many illustrated with woodcuts, of which the finest examples are undoubtedly by the early sixteenth-century Dutch artist Lucas Van Leyden. One of the best known stories, much favoured by illustrators, is 'Virgil in the Basket', in which Virgil, enamoured of the Emperor of Rome's daughter, agrees to her plan to climb into a basket one night and be drawn up the wall of the tower where she lives to her room. She, however, leaves him suspended half way up, much to the amusement of the Roman people the following morning.

This is all, however, folklore, not Virgil. As the legends had spread wider and wider, the Virgil of living legend had become less and less individual, less and less recognizable as the learned and civilized Roman poet. His voice could still faintly be heard in the popular mediaeval romances of the Troy story – which, however, depended as much on the Cretan writer Dictys and the Phrygian Dares as on Virgil, and probably even more on Homer – and it was left to the educated minority to continue the admiration of the real Virgil.

7

VIRGIL'S IMITATORS

VIRGIL WAS BY FAR the most influential of the Latin poets. His mastery of the epic form, his supreme skill with words, and his understanding and sympathetic portrayal of human emotions ensured his place among the greatest of all poets; the *Georgics* and the *Eclogues* have been admired and imitated over the centuries, and the *Aeneid* has remained a source of inspiration to succeeding generations of poets – and to composers and artists. His influence on his fellow-poets is obvious from the frequency with which they quote him overtly and make unmistakable references to his work, and his successors in time have often felt that he was one of them, in some way alive and sharing their calling, just as the twentieth-century Scottish poet Hugh Macdiarmid felt himself to be in communion with the 'makars' or Scottish poets of the sixteenth century.

During and shortly after Virgil's lifetime, we know that the Emperor Augustus admired him, Maecenas, the leading literary patron of Rome, poured praise upon him, his fellow-poet Horace loved him – in his *Odes* (1.3.8) he calls Virgil 'half of my own life' – and the poet Silius Italicus worshipped him. Silius records that he made an annual pilgrimage to Virgil's tomb, as if to a temple, and he took trouble to ensure that the tomb was properly conserved. Statius, the Latin poet whom Dante thought a fit companion in his travels through Purgatory, finishes his epic poem *Thebaid* with the lines:

Virgil's Imitators

Vive, precor, nec tu divinam Aeneida tenta
sed longe sequere, et vestigia semper adora.

Live, I pray, do not try to rival the divine *Aeneid*, but
follow at a distance, and worship its footprints.

Ovid, the last of the great poets of the Latin 'Golden Age',
who had indeed seen the famed Virgil, uses many of Virgil's
phrases and techniques. In his *Heroides* 7, based on *Aeneid* 4, he
enjoys himself by composing a letter from Dido to Aeneas.
Exiled by the Emperor Augustus and his verse censored, Ovid
tries to excuse himself for having written poems about love by
saying in his autobiographical poem *Tristia* that the most
popular part of the *Aeneid* was the story of Dido in which

> *ille tuae felix Aeneidis auctor*
> *Contulit in Tyrios arma virumque toros.*
>
> (*Tristia* 2. 533–534)

The successful author of your Aeneid brought his 'arms
and the man' to the feast at Carthage [i.e., to Dido's feast
and Dido's bed].

The epic poets Lucan and Valerius Flaccus of the first
century AD were equally steeped in Virgil, and Juvenal, who
published his first satirical verses in about AD 110, used
Virgilian diction to bring the high epic style to satire. In the
fourth century, both the pagan poet Claudian and the Christian
poet Prudentius adapted Virgilian rhythms and phrases for
their very different purposes.

Christian poets could not indeed ignore Virgil even if the
Church might denounce the pagan gods described in his poems
and find parts of his work not entirely edifying. (The Jesuits
banned *Aeneid* 4, describing Dido's love and suicide, from their

school curricula.) Juvencus, who lived in the middle of the fourth century, wrote an epic on the Gospel story, and Dracontius over a century later wrote an epic on the loss of Paradise and its recovery, which pointed the way for Milton. Avitus, who died about 526, wrote an epic on the Creation, taking the story up to the Crossing of the Red Sea, and his versification owes much to Virgil. There are numerous clear echoes of Virgil's work: in the Garden of Eden there is eternal spring – *hic ver assidum* – as there is in Virgil's praise of Italy in the second *Georgic*. A few lines further on Avitus recalls another passage from Virgil's praise of Italy in which Virgil writes:

> *quid tibi odorato referam sudantia ligno*
> *balsamaque et bacas semper frondentis acanthi.*

Why should I tell you of the balsam that seeps out of fragrant trees, and the 'berries' of evergreen acanthus [i.e., gum arabic].

Avitus puts it this way:

> *Illic desudans fragrantia balsama ramus*
> *perpetuum promit pingui de stipite fluxum.*
> *tum si forte levis movit spiramina ventus,*
> *flatibus exiguis lenique impulsa susurro*
> *dives silva tremit foliis et flore salubri*
> *qui sparsus late suaves dispensat odores.*

There fragrant balsam oozes perpetually from the bough's fat stem. Then whenever a light breeze blows, the rich wood is stirred by the slightest puff and gentlest whisper, its leaves and health-giving flowers quivering, and far and wide dispenses its sweet odours.

Virgil's Imitators

In the Dark Ages that followed the collapse of the Roman Empire, there were fewer opportunities to imitate Virgil, as far as we know, but with the revival of learning in the time of Charlemagne, scholars looked to the classical authors for inspiration. Walahfrid Strabo writing at Reichenau in the ninth century employs many of the metrical devices that Virgil himself used in his *Hortulus*, a poem of 444 very respectable hexameters, and he probably chose to write on horticulture because it was a subject that Virgil deliberately did not treat in the *Georgics*. Walahfrid's first paragraph ends in a 'golden line', imitative of Virgil, in the grammatical form: adjective (1), adjective (2), verb, noun (1), noun (2) – *inlita ferventi creverunt tela veneno* ('the weapons smeared with deadly poison grew large').

In the tenth century, Ekkehard, Dean of St Gall, wrote a lively epic called *Waltharius* which has many verbal echoes of Virgil, with some nice humorous touches. It tells the story of Waltharius and Hildgund, royal hostages at the court of Attila the Hun, who elope to the Vosges. After their escape, Attila spends a sleepless night, which is described in terms reminiscent of Dido abandoned by Aeneas. The epic is resolved when Waltharius defeats three warriors sent by Attila to bring him and Hildgund back.

An epic in ten books which enjoyed enormous success was the *Alexandreis* of Walter of Lille, or of Chatillon, who lived from about 1135 to after 1189. His poem of 5500 Latin hexameters, half as long as the *Aeneid*, tells the story of Alexander the Great based on the history of Quintus Curtius, a good choice of subject since Alexander's fame was worldwide and he was even the hero of many legends in the Islamic world, where his name took the form Iskander. Inevitably Walter was influenced by Virgil's great epic and in the prose prologue to the *Alexandreis*, Walter modestly pays tribute to Virgil:

97

Virgil through the Ages

I do not consider myself better than the poet of Mantua, whose works which surpass human genius were disparaged by the tongues of carping poets, and once he was dead they presumed to belittle the man whom no mortal could equal, at least as long as he was alive. But our own Jerome, as learned as he is Christian, who was accustomed to answer his detractors in his prefaces, clearly makes it understood that there is no place where even a man of such exalted reputation is safe from the knives of envy.

Despite Walter's contemporary reputation, only one of his lines is familiar now – it has passed into the proverb 'Between Scylla and Charybdis'. Virgil's Aeneas was strongly urged not to steer a course between these two famous monsters, but to go the long way round Sicily. In Walter's epic, the line is:

Incidis in Scyllam cupiens vitare Charybdim.

When you seek to avoid Charybdis, you fall into Scylla.

Shakespeare used the expression in *The Merchant of Venice* when Launcelot says jokingly to Jessica, 'When I shun Scylla, your father, I fall into Charybdis, your mother'; and Walter Scott in *St Ronan's Well* has a mock-heroic passage in which the nabob, Mr Touchwood, makes a considerable circuit to avoid the open sewer of the village, and by that means falls upon Scylla (the river) as he seeks to avoid Charybdis (the sewer).

The fourteenth-century Italian poet and scholar Petrarch, the first humanist, wrote, like Virgil, ten *Eclogues* and one epic poem, *Africa*, among his other works. He spent some of his life at the papal court at Avignon and travelled widely in search of lost classical texts. In his *Eclogues* he treated historical and autobiographical themes in an allegorical manner, as Virgil was thought to have done, and possibly did in part. For example, Petrarch's second *Eclogue* features two shepherds singing competitively about the death of Argus (i.e., Robert of Anjou, Petrarch's chief patron, who died in 1343); likewise in Virgil's fifth *Eclogue* two shepherds sing competitively about the death of Daphnis. (Some people have supposed that Daphnis was Julius Caesar, murdered five years before the *Eclogues* were published, and this is the interpretation adopted by Petrarch, although Virgil keeps us guessing.) Virgil's first shepherd, Mopsus, sings of how the hills and woods tell that the lions of Africa mourn Daphnis, and Menalcas, in his rival song, addresses Daphnis as a god. Petrarch's first shepherd laments the loss of one who renewed the sacred games and who, while he was leader, made the wood safe and drove away the clouds. The second shepherd celebrates Argus's prowess at hunting and sings that he has departed never to return, looking down on his now leaderless people from high in heaven.

Petrarch's epic, in nine books and still unfinished at his death, is about the Second Punic War, in which the Romans defeated the Carthaginians and conquered Africa with the judicious assistance of Masinissa, a prince of Numidia. This is the great period of Roman history when Hannibal, Rome's most formidable adversary, reached the gates of the city itself, and Scipio Africanus – the hero of Petrarch's epic – won his reputation as a military commander. (He also, it is said, inaugurated the fashion for daily shaving.) Petrarch took his material from the Roman historian Livy who was born about ten years after Virgil and who had a particular interest for Petrarch. It was Petrarch who was instrumental in rediscovering a long-lost section of Livy's history of Rome.

It is not too fanciful to see the resemblances between Scipio and Aeneas, although Scipio is completely honourable and it is his non-Roman ally, Masinissa, who has the part of the cad who abandons his love. There is a clear parallel between

Syphax's wife Sophonisba and Dido (and of course the historical Cleopatra). Sophonisba, a Carthaginian princess, persuades her husband Syphax to renounce his alliance with Rome, drive out Masinissa, and join the Carthaginian cause. Scipio's general, Laelius, with Masinissa's help, defeats and captures Syphax and Sophonisba, and she sets out to bewitch her captor. She succeeds so well that she and Masinissa are married the day they meet and celebrate their dubious nuptials in an abandoned castle – a romantic detail added by Petrarch to Livy's briefer but still romantic account. Masinissa promises not to hand his new wife over to the Romans, a promise which puts him in a dilemma. When Scipio refuses to approve the adulterous union, insisting that Sophonisba be taken to Rome as a prisoner, Masinissa, like Aeneas, is torn between the claims of love and duty. The solution he finds is extremely painful – to send Sophonisba poison as the only way to escape Roman captivity. 'I accept the gift,' says Sophonisba, 'if there is nothing better from a husband, but I should die more easily if it were not also my wedding.' Petrarch makes her utter prophetic curses on both Scipio and Masinissa, again like Dido, and as she dies her spirit flees violently to Hades (*Tartareasque petit violentus spiritus umbras*). This line is a forcible reminder of the last line of the *Aeneid*: *vitaque cum gemitu fugit indignata sub umbras* (with a groan Turnus's life fled protesting to the shades below), a line which Virgil had already used to describe the death of the other principal warrior enemy of Aeneas, the Amazon Camilla. Petrarch, by this allusion, is comparing Sophonisba to Camilla, both of whom were active enemies of Rome to their dying day.

Although Petrarch's epic did not attain the success he hoped for, his *Eclogues* did. They were collected together with the *Eclogues* of Virgil, Calpurnius (who lived in the first century AD) and Nemesianus (of the third century): Harley MS 2578 is such a collection, and it also includes the Centos of Proba and

Ausonius. Similar collections were printed and the Harley manuscript may depend, in whole or in part, on a printed edition.

The Eclogue was further developed by the Renaissance Latin poets. Mantuan (whose real name was Battista Spagnuoli but who was given the nickname by which he is generally known because he spent most of his life at Mantua) used it for didactic purposes. He was a prolific poet of reformist tendency, which made him popular north of the Alps, but his bitter satires on the corruption of the papal court (e.g., *Eclogue* 9) can hardly have endeared him to the Pope and his supporters. Jacopo Sannazaro introduced a very successful variation in his *Eclogues*: shepherds were replaced by fishermen and the heroine, Galatea, appears more frequently than other ladies.

Amaryllis, a favourite of Virgil's, kept her place in Renaissance love poems and was joined by Neaera, an unknown girl from Naples, to whom the soldier and Latin poet Michael Marullus (born in Constantinople in *c.*1453) addressed many love lyrics. Milton in his youth knew all these poems well, and as he says in *Lycidas* he was tempted to continue the tradition of Latin poetry:

> Were it not better done as others use,
> To sport with Amaryllis in the shade,
> Or with the tangles of Neaera's hair?

However, he decided instead to give up writing Latin pastorals and try 'fresh woods and pastures new'.

Another traditional part of the Latin poet's armoury which could not be ignored by later poets was the 'purple patch' exemplified by the praise of Italy in the second book of Virgil's *Georgics*. In this tradition, the Scots humanist George Buchanan wrote praises of Scotland in his *Epithalamion*, a poem written for the wedding in April 1558 of Mary, Queen of Scots, to

Francis, Dauphin of France. It is entirely appropriate to the subject, and there are interesting similarities with Virgil's treatment. Virgil recites the agricultural and mineral wealth of Italy, and then extols its martial virtues in the person of its famous heroes. He conjures up a dream of a united Italy, free of war and civil strife. Buchanan says of Scotland, 'I shall not recount its acres of fertile land, its glens and waters that produce abundant cattle and fish, its copper- and lead-laden fields, its hills bearing gold and iron, its rivers flowing from mineral veins (*deque metalliferis manantia flumina venis*), and then he, like Virgil, goes on to boast of his countrymen's prowess in war. The fervour in Buchanan's verse reflects the centuries-old battle of the Scots to keep the English out, and he recalls the climax of Scotland's valour which, ironically, is when they alone stopped the Romans from occupying their country, enduring hunger, cold and heat, despising life itself to keep their good name and to maintain their freedom – *gens una vetustis/Sedibus antiqua sub libertate resedit* (a single nation settled in its ancient home in long-standing freedom).

The didactic rural atmosphere of Virgil's *Georgics* came alive above all in the tale of Syphilis, a Latin poem written in about 1530 by the Veronese scholar and physician Girolamo Fracastoro. The shepherd Syphilis neglects to worship Apollo and in consequence is visited with the disease that bears his name. He is healed by a decoction of the sacred tree Guiacum, a remedy used by the people of Haiti, where the disease was supposed to have originated. The ingenious combination of medical research and geographical discovery in the New World brought this poem deserved success and the great sixteenth-century French scholar Joseph Justus Scaliger described it as the finest poem since Virgil.

Milton, probably the last successful epic poet in English, uses many of the traditional devices of epic poetry. Like Virgil who took several years to find the tale of Aeneas, Milton had

trouble in finding a subject grand enough for epic treatment
which at the same time had enough points of contact with his
own times and situation. He first considered the King Arthur
story but then rejected it, and settled on the story of the Fall of
Man, which could not be a grander subject but which has the
disadvantage that all the combatants are immortal, so that the
battles between the Devil's fallen angels and the hosts of heaven
cannot have a fatal outcome.

In *Paradise Lost* and *Paradise Regained*, Milton uses the
familiar epic device of placing Hell in remoteness. Homer had
said that the pit into which Zeus threatened to throw disobe-
dient gods was as far below the earth as the heavens were above
the earth, and Virgil had placed Tartarus, the place of torment
for sinners, twice as far below the Underworld (where Aeneas
was then standing) as Olympus above the earth. Milton goes
one better and increases the factor to three:

> Such place Eternal Justice had prepar'd
> For those rebellious, here thir Pris'n ordaind
> In utter darkness, and thir portion set
> As far remov'd from God and light of Heav'n
> As from the Center thrice to th'utmost Pole.

Another traditional technique was to make verse out of a
list of romantic names. Homer has a catalogue of the ships that
took part in the expedition to Troy, and Virgil too showed
himself master of this technique, whether listing combatants or
the companions of Neptune:

> *laeva tenet Thetis et Melite Panopeaque virgo*
> *Nisaee Spioque Thaliaque Cymodoceque*
>
> (*Aeneid* 5. 825–826)

Milton follows the tradition in *Paradise Lost* when he speaks of all the knights who:

> Jousted in Aspramont or Montalban,
> Damasco, or Marocco, or Trebisond,
> Or whom Biserta sent from Afric shore
> When Charlemain with all his Peerage fell
> By Fontarabbia.

Even today the tradition is alive in poetry, as the Scottish nationalist poet Hugh Macdiarmid shows in his astonishingly successful catalogue of romantic-sounding names of rocks and stones in *On a Raised Beach*.

The treatment of these rhetorical commonplaces definitely suggests a continuity of tradition from the very beginning of epic poetry, but it is Virgil's own monstrous Scylla in the *Aeneid* Book 3 which is unmistakably imitated both in Spenser's Errour in the *Faerie Queene* and in Milton's Sin in *Paradise Lost*:

> Halfe like a serpent horribly displaide,
> But th'other halfe did womans shape retaine,
> Most lothsom, filthie, foule, and full of vile disdaine.
> And as she lay vpon the durtie ground,
> Her huge long taile her den all ouerspred,
> Yet was in knots and many boughtes vpwound,
> Pointed with mortall sting. Of her there bred
> A thousand yong ones, which she dayly fed,
> Sucking vpon her poisonous dugs, eachone
> Of sundry shapes, yet all ill fauored:
> Soone as that vncouth light vpon them shone,
> Into her mouth they crept, and suddain all were gone.
>
> *(Faerie Queene* I. I.14–I5)

Virgil's Imitators

The one seemd Woman to the waist, and fair,
But ended foul in many a scaly fold
Voluminous and vast, a Serpent armd
With mortal sting: about her middle round
A cry of Hell Hounds never ceasing barkd
With wide Cerberean mouths full loud, and rung
A hideous Peal; yet when they list, would creep,
If ought disturbd thir noise, into her womb,
And kennel there, yet there still barkd and howld
Within unseen.

(Paradise Lost 2. 650–659)

This is very close to Virgil:

At Scyllam caecis cohibet spelunca latebris
ora exsertantem et navis in saxa trahentem.
prima hominis facies et pulchro pectore virgo
pube tenus, postrema immani corpore pistrix
delphinum caudas utero commissa luporum.
praestat Trinacrii metas lustrare Pachyni
cessantem, longos et circumflectere cursus,
quam semel informem vasto vidisse sub antro
Scyllam et caeruleis canibus resonantia saxa.

(Aeneid 3. 424–432)

A cave holds Scylla in its blind darkness; she darts out her
mouths and drags ships on to the rocks. At first she looks
human, a girl with beautiful breast as far as the waist, but
below a sea-monster of horrible appearance, with a belly
of wolves and a tail of dolphins. It is far better to go the
long way round Sicily, with all that delay, than to have
once seen frightful Scylla in her vast submarine cavern and
to have once seen the rocks that echo the sea-green dogs.

In lines 404–409 of the first *Georgic* Virgil mentions another Scylla, the daughter of Nisus, King of Megara. For love she betrayed her city by cutting off her father's magic lock of hair, and for this crime she was turned into a lark constantly pursued by a sparrowhawk. The legend is treated at length in a poem called *Ciris* ('The Lark'), which was long thought to be by Virgil. Edmund Spenser certainly believed it was a genuine Virgilian poem, and borrowed from it many details in the story of Britomartis the warrior princess in *The Faerie Queene* Book 3, Canto 2.

The eighteenth century did not produce any great epics but Virgil's *Aeneid* was widely influential, his *Eclogues* produced many imitations – Alexander Pope's pastoral poems, for example – and the didacticism of the *Georgics* struck a responsive chord among gentlemen proud to be thought farmers. Virgil was seen to embody the aristocratic virtues, and the georgic proved to be an extremely productive genre. The parallel with Virgil's *Georgics* is particularly close in John Philips' *Cyder* (1708), which combines practical instruction in an agricultural subject not handled by Virgil with a mock-heroic account of the destruction of a legendary city overcome by an earthquake. The imitation of Virgil becomes less direct as the genre developed along its own lines. For example, in James Thomson's *The Seasons* (1730), the construction is less imitative of Virgil, although there are, inevitably, verbal echoes, and the references to the swan are at the very least in the long tradition that goes back to Virgil:

> The stately-sailing swan
> Gives out his snowy plumage to the gale,
> And, arching proud his neck, with oary feet
> Bears forward fierce, and guards his osier-isle,
> Protective of his young.

Virgil's Imitators

William Wordsworth represents a further development of the genre in the nineteenth century. In both Virgil and Wordsworth there is something numinous and divine in nature, but in Virgil this is an expression of the gods who control human life, while in Wordsworth nature itself seems to be the divinity. The rise of the modern city as a result of the Industrial Revolution makes the ideal rural life even more unreal, but in a further continuation of the genre the other and Scottish-born James Thomson was able to use the contrast with the ideal rural life to add point to the terror in his poem *The City of Dreadful Night* (1880).

The *Aeneid* was on the whole not greatly admired by the Romantic poets, who saw Aeneas as colourless and weak, and odious in his behaviour towards Dido. They did, however, appreciate its pathos and sensitivity to the 'tears in things' and later in the nineteenth century leading critics and poets like Matthew Arnold and Alfred Tennyson were deeply moved by the tenderness which they felt was the special characteristic of Virgil. Tennyson paid tribute to the Latin poet on the occasion of the nineteenth centenary of Virgil's death and speaks in his poem, *To Virgil*, of 'all the charm of all the Muses often flowering in a lonely word', and 'thou majestic in thy sadness at the doubtful doom of humankind'. He ends:

> I salute thee, Mantovano,
>> I that loved thee since my day began,
> Wielder of the stateliest measure
>> Ever moulded by the lips of man.

Although it is among poets that Virgil's imitators are obviously to be found, his influence has not been limited to poetry. With the revival of classical learning in the Renaissance, he and the other classical writers became a source of inspiration to painters, and a sense of classical antiquity informs the work of such artists as Claude, Poussin, Rubens and, later, Turner and Richard Wilson. Claude in particular shared Virgil's deep love of the countryside of Campania, so strongly depicted in the *Georgics*, and often took Virgil's work as the subject of his paintings. His contemporary and fellow-countryman Poussin used Virgil's story of Orpheus and Eurydice as the title of one of his finest landscapes, and both this story and that of Dido and Aeneas have also been used by composers, among them Gluck and Purcell.

The most ambitious translation of Virgil into music is, however, undoubtedly *The Trojans* of Hector Berlioz who all his life felt a strong emotional response to Virgil. His huge opera, based on Books 2 and 4 of the *Aeneid*, was first performed in Paris in 1863 in a severely cut version but had to wait until 1969, a century after the composer's death, for its first complete performance – at Covent Garden in French.

It was Berlioz's *The Trojans* that brought the twentieth-century British artist Michael Ayrton to Virgil, and what fascinated him in particular was the description of the series of reliefs at the Sibyl's Temple in the beginning of Book 6 of the *Aeneid*. Here is the story of Daedalus the maze-maker, the Minotaur, the escape by flight from Crete, and the impious Icarus who flew too near the sun and paid the penalty. Ayrton felt compelled by a mysterious revelation to rewrite the myth in his books *The Testament of Daedalus* and *The Maze-Maker*, and to cast in bronze the characters and incidents in the myth. He, like others before him, felt Virgil's presence at his elbow, as if like some diminutive Dante he had been led by Virgil into the rock at Cumae and through the Labyrinth of Earth.

8

VIRGIL IN ENGLISH

In order to make Virgil part of the living tradition of each generation we must translate him afresh, not only for those who have no Latin, but also for those who can read him in the original. No translation can do full justice to the original, hence the Italian aphorism, *tradduttore traditore* – 'the translator is a traitor'. Nevertheless we must make the attempt. How shall we translate? Which aspect emphasize? What purpose aim at? Is it for reading? speaking? singing? What liberties can we take with the language? Verse or prose? Which metre? To take an example from elsewhere, the Psalms in the Authorized Version of the Bible read aloud sonorously and fluently. On the other hand the version in the Scottish Psalter is written in common metre, or ballad metre, a four-line stanza alternately eight and six syllables to the line. This verse form was a popular medium for songs, and despite its awkward word order this version is successfully adapted for singing by the people. I wonder which version of the twenty-third Psalm is most widely known today?

Let us now look at Virgil as he has been translated into the English language, remembering that by 1553, when the first English translation was printed, over forty partial or complete translations had already been made into other European languages. We shall ignore prose translations on the grounds that they abandon all hope of reproducing the poetry of the original, and begin by looking at several strategies that have been used by translators. We can start very early indeed, for Chaucer incorporated in two of his poems fairly close translations of passages of the *Aeneid*. In his *Hous of Fame* he translated the first few lines of the *Aeneid*:

> I will now sing, if that I can,
> The armès, and also the man,
> That first came, through destinee,
> Fugitive of Troy country,
> In Itaile, with full muchè pyne,   (pyne: pain)
> Unto the strandès of Lavyne.

The spelling is modernized, but remember that e's which are silent in modern English can be sounded, if needed, to make the verse metrical. (These sounded e's are marked with a dot above them.)

In his *Legend of Good Women* he included a rendering of Aeneas's meeting with his mother Venus in *Aeneid* 1. 320–340:

> A bow in hand, and arrows haddè she,
> Her clothès cutted were unto the knee;
> But she was yet the fairest creature,
> That ever was y-formèd by nature;
> And Aeneas and Achates she grette,
> And thus she to 'em spake, when she 'em met.
> 'Saw ye,' quod she, 'as ye han walkèd wide,   (han: have)
> Any of my sistren walkè you beside,
> With any wildè boar or other beast
> That they han hunted to, in this forest,
> Y-tuckèd up, with arrows in her case?'
> 'Nay soothly, lady,' quod this Aeneas,
> But by thy beauty, as it thinketh me,
> Thou mightest never earthly woman be,

But Phoebus' sister art thou, as I guess.
And if so be that thou be a goddess,
Have mercy on our labour and our woe.'
'I am no goddess, soothly,' quod she tho;
'For maidens walken in this country here,
With arrows and with bow, in this manner.
This is the reign of Libye, there ye been
Of which that Dido lady is and queen.'

This is vivid free-flowing narrative; what it does not convey is the breathless surprise of Aeneas as he recognizes Venus as a goddess. Chaucer uses the heroic couplet, considered the most appropriate medium for narrative verse until Dryden and later. It has the disadvantage when translating Virgil's verse paragraphs that there is a stop at the end of each line.

A century or so later Gawin Douglas, Bishop of Dunkeld in Perthshire, made the first complete translation of the *Aeneid* into English; as far as we can tell, he made no use of the French translation of St Gelais. He finished his twelve years' work on 22 July 1513, but it was not printed until 1553. His translation is rougher than Chaucer's, and he complains of the limitations of the 'bad harsk Scottis' that he has to use. He aims at accuracy, but makes some expansions and omissions. Douglas's translation emphasizes the idea that the just prince has a right to the absolute obedience of his subjects, a constant Renaissance theme, just as in the eighteenth century the *Aeneid* was seen as embodying the ideal constitutional monarch. Both these views illustrate the continuing relevance of Virgil – to us, I suspect, he represents civilization threatened by a rising tide of barbarism and inhumanity.

There was another reason for Douglas to make his translation: indignation at a book printed by William Caxton in 1490, *The Eneydos of Vyrgyle*. Douglas devotes 130 lines to Caxton's faults and complains that Caxton's work has no more to do with Virgil than the devil with St Augustine. Two thirds of it are given over to Dido's love and death, and the rest is either brutally abbreviated or totally omitted. To quote Douglas, the last six books:

> Which containis strong battles and wars
> This ilk Caxton so blately lets o'erslip   (blately: blatantly)
> I hold my tongue for shame, biting my lip.

('Containis', a plural form, can be pronounced in two or three syllables according to the metre; the past participle form -it in the same way makes a syllable or not to fit the metre.) Douglas also complains that 'Caxton for dred they should his lippis scald/Durst never touch' Virgil's brilliant decorative style.

The Eneydos of Vyrgyle is in fact a translation by Caxton himself of a French fourteenth-century romance, and it bears as little resemblance to Virgil's poem as Douglas says it does. One example will suffice: the last three lines of *Aeneid* 12:

> *hoc dicens ferrum adverso sub pectore condit*
> *fervidus. ast illi solvuntur frigore membra*
> *vitaque cum gemitu fugit indignata sub umbras.*

> Saying this he plunged his sword into his opponent's breast, violently. And the other's limbs relax with cold, and with a groan his life flies complaining to the shades below.

These are flatly abbreviated thus:

> And anon he shoved his sword through the body of him, whereout his soul departed.

It has none of the pathos or the tension of Virgil, nor the

violence of Aeneas's blow, nor the sadness of Turnus's parting soul.

For all that, Caxton's book kept Virgil's name and his epic alive in the minds of the people. And it has another claim on our interest. In the preface Caxton discusses the problems of translation, and in particular what sort of English he should use – the elaborate style or the plain style. He had observed that the English spoken when he was young was different from that currently spoken, and that there were great differences between the dialects of English. He tells the story of how some merchants, London friends of his, were on their way to Zealand by sea. They were becalmed off Kent and landed for fresh provisions. One of the merchants, whose name was Sheffield, knocked at a house and asked the woman of the house for eggs. She did not understand him and said that she could not speak French. Mr Sheffield was understandably annoyed because he could not speak French either. At last communication was established when someone said that what he wanted was 'eyren', and then the woman said that she understood him well. So we can see that the English of Kent was different enough from the English of London to cause difficulties.

Douglas's verse has a no-nonsense quality about it. It is plain and direct, for example, he translates *Aeneas laetitia exsultans* as 'hoppit for joy, he was so glad'. He uses the rhymed heroic couplet, like Chaucer, and some parts, like the sea-scenes, are so vigorous that in *How to Read* Ezra Pound provocatively described Douglas's poem as better than the original, in that Douglas had seen the sea, and in the *ABC of Reading* he said 'in such passages as this [the storm in *Aeneid* 1] I get considerably more pleasure from the Bishop of Dunkeld than from the original highly-cultured but non-seafaring author'.

Here is the storm in question:

Virgil through the Ages

> stridens Aquilone procella
> velum adversa ferit, fluctusque ad sidera tollit.
> franguntur remi, tum prora avertit et undis
> dat latus, insequitur cumulo praeruptus aquae mons.
> hi summo in fluctu pendent; his unda dehiscens
> terram inter fluctus aperit, furit aestus harenis.
>
> (*Aeneid* 1. 102–107)

Douglas translates each word, and his text is longer than Virgil's, but admirably vigorous:

A blustering bub out from the north braying	(bub: squall)
Gan ower the foreship in the backsail ding	(ding: strike)
And to the sternis up the flood gan cast.	(sternis: stars)
The aris, hatches and the tackles brast,	(aris: oars; brast: burst)
The shipps stevin frawart her went gan wryth,	(The ship's stem off her course did twist)
And turnit her broadside to the wallis swyth.	(swyth: at once)
Heich as a hill the jaw of water brak	(heich: high)
And in a heap cam on them with a swack.	
Some hesit hovering on the wallis height	(hesit: hoisted)
And some the swouching sea so low gart licht	(gart licht: made to alight)
Them seemit the earth openit amid the flood –	
The stour up bullerit sand as it were wood.	(bullerit: boiled; wood: mad)

In *Notes on the Elizabethan Classicists*, Pound had taken a more moderate line: 'I am inclined to think that Douglas gets more poetry out of Virgil than any other translator. At least he gives one a clue to Dante's respect for the Mantuan.' Here is Aeneas meeting Venus:

For Venus after the guise and manner there,
An active bow upon her shoulder bare,

Virgil in English

As scho had been a wild hunteress,   (scho: she)
With wind waving her hairis loosit of tress
Her skirt kiltit till her bare knee,
And first of other, unto them spake she:
'How, say me, youngkers, saw ye walking here
By aventure any of my sisters dear,
The case of arrows tachit by her side,   (tachit: attached)
And clad in to the spotted lynx hide,
Or with loud cry following the chase
After the foamy boar, in their solace?'

In 1558, five years after Douglas's translation was published, Thomas Phaer's translation of *Aeneid* 1–7 was published in London. The whole *Aeneid* was not printed until 1582, completed by Thomas Twyne. Phaer's verse swings, or more often limps leadenly along, in the popular ballad metre, but with two lines combined in a single line of fourteen syllables:

> For hunterlike her bow she bare, her locks went with the
>   wind
> Behind her back, and tuckt she was that naked was her
>   knee.
> She called to them and said, 'Good sirs, I pray you did you
>   see
> To stray this way as ye have come, my sisters any one?
> With quiver bound that in the chase of some wild beast are
>   gone?
> Or with a cry pursueth apace the foamy boar to pain?'

Phaer's fourteen-syllable line nearly corresponds in length to Virgil's hexameter, but English needs more syllables than Latin, so Phaer needs somewhat more lines than Virgil. Compared with Douglas, Phaer's verse is heavy-going, and the prospect of reading 10,000 lines like this must daunt the stoutest heart.

Several attempts have been made to approximate more closely to the Latin hexameter than Phaer's fourteener. Perhaps the most ambitious, or the most foolhardy, was that of Richard Stanyhurst, who in 1582 published the first four books of the *Aeneid* in an English quantitative hexameter. It was a brave attempt to render Virgil whole, leaving nothing out, but the effect is irredeemably comic, for example the beginning of the poem:

> Now manhood and garboils I chaunt, and martiall horror.
> I blaze thee captain first from Troy city repairing,
> Like wandring pilgrim to famosed Italie trudging
> And coast of Lavyn.

Following the rules of Latin scansion his syllables are long if they have a long vowel (as in 'like') or if a short vowel is followed by two consonants, not necessarily in the same word (so, for example, 'pilgrim' makes two long syllables). In the next extract, Aeneas's meeting with Venus, he uses the spelling 'shee' to indicate a long syllable, as Milton was to do later.

> Shee bare on her shoulders her bow bent aptly like huntress,
> Down the wind tracing trailed her disheveled hairlocks;
> Tuck'd to the knee naked; thus first shee forged her errand
> 'Ho sirs, perceived you some maiden company straggling,
> Of my dear sisters with quiver closely begirded
> Rearing with shoutcry some boar, some sanglier ugly?'

Stanyhurst's verse was much criticized – Thomas Nashe spoke contemptuously of his 'foul lumbering boisterous wallowing measure' – and certainly his predilection for obscure words spoils even his more successful passages. Perhaps some of the pathos of the beginning of Book 2 of the *Aeneid* is, however, detectable in the following lines

> What ruter of Dolopans were so cruel hearted in
>   hearkning,
> What curst Myrmidons, what karne of cankred Ulysses,
> That void of all weeping could hear so mortal an hazard?

In 1654 John Ogilby published his own translation of the whole of Virgil. His translation is uninspired, but what distinguishes this splendid edition is the hundred 'sculptures' or engravings designed by Francis Clein and engraved by Wenceslas Hollar and Pierre Lambert, all three of whom came to England to make their fortunes and to escape from the miseries of the religious wars of the continent. The plates were re-used in Ogilby's edition of Virgil in Latin in 1658, and used again in the first edition of Dryden's translation of 1697. In this edition the figure of Aeneas was given William III's royal nose, and what a noble nose it is too. This was a compliment to the king, and many of the plates were dedicated to members of the royal family. The 1654, 1658 and 1697 editions were all in folio size, but a subsequent edition of Dryden was much smaller, so that the engravings were drastically reduced, losing much of their power in the process. Here is Aeneas's meeting with Venus in Ogilby's version of 1654 (he published an earlier version in 1649):

> For, as they used, she wore a handsome bow,
> And to the wanton winds exposed her hair;
> Tucked to her knee her flowing garments were.
> And first to them she calls; Have you, I pray,
> Seen any of my sisters pass this way?
> In lynx skins girt, thay cast light quivers o're,
> Or heard them hunting of the foamie boar?

We can recognize some turns of speech from earlier translations.

However all other translations were quite put in the shade
by Dryden. His stated aim was 'to make Virgil speak such
English as he would himself have spoken if he had been born in
England, and in this present age'. In these terms Dryden's
version must be counted a triumphant success. Here is Aeneas's
meeting with Venus:

> A huntress in her habit and her mien,
> Her dress a maid, her air confessed a queen.
> Bare were her knees, and knots her garments bind;
> Loose was her hair, and wantoned in the wind;
> Her hand sustained a bow, her quiver hung behind.
> She seemed a virgin of the Spartan blood:
> With such array Harpalice bestrode
> Her Thracian courser, and outstrip'd the rapid flood.
> 'Ho! strangers! have you lately seen,' she said,
> 'One of my sisters, like myself arrayed;
> Who crossed the lawn, or in the forest strayed?
> A painted quiver at her back she bore;
> Varied with spots, a lynx's hide she wore;
> And at full cry pursu'd the tusky boar?'
> Thus Venus: Thus her Son replied agen;
> 'None of your sisters have we heard or seen,
> O virgin! or what other name you bear
> Above that style; O more than mortal fair!
> Your voice and mien celestial birth betray!'

But even Dryden had difficulty in keeping up this standard
over such a long poem as the *Aeneid*, not to mention the
Eclogues and *Georgics*:

From the beginning of the first *Georgic* to the end of the

last *Aeneid*, I found the difficulty of translation growing on me in every succeeding book: for Virgil, above all poets, had a stock, which I may call almost inexhaustible, of figurative, elegant, and sounding words. I, who inherit but a small portion of his genius, and write in a language so much inferior to the Latin, have found it very painful to vary phrases, when the same sense returns upon me. Even he himself, whether out of necessity or choice, has so often expressed the same thing in the same words, and often repeated two or three whole verses, which he had used before. Words are not so easily coined as money; and yet we see that the credit, not only of banks, but of exchequers, cracks, when little comes in, and much goes out. Virgil called upon me in every line for some new word; and I paid so long that I was almost bankrupt; so that the latter end must needs be more burdensome than the beginning or the middle; and consequently the twelfth Aeneid cost me double the time of the first and second.

Dryden's enormous success did not prevent later generations from trying to overcome the difficulties of such verbal inflation. The British Library's Catalogue lists thirty translators of the *Aeneid* from Dryden's time to 1952. In earlier chapters we have seen several samples of C. Day Lewis's excellent translation. Let us look at two nineteenth-century versions, those of Conington and Morris. John Conington was a classical scholar whose work on Virgil is still useful. His *Aeneid* came out in 1866, in jaunty eight-syllable lines. This metre gives a natural, lively rhythm, but it is difficult to achieve an effect of solemnity with it. Here is Aeneas meeting Venus, where we can see that the description of Venus is lively and not bound too closely to the original, but Aeneas's reply seems awkward and flat, with unnatural word-order.

Virgil through the Ages

When in the bosom of the wood
Before him, lo, his mother stood.
In mien and gear a Spartan maid
Or like Harpalyce arrayed,
Who tires fleet coursers in the chase,
And heads the swiftest streams of Thrace.
Slung from her shoulders hangs a bow.
Loose to the wind her tresses flow;
Bare was her knee; her mantle's fold
The gathering of a knot controlled.
And 'Saw ye, youths,' she asks them, 'Say,
One of my sisters here astray,
A silvan quiver at her side,
And for a scarf a lynx's hide?
Or pressing on the wild boar's track,
With upraised dart and voiceful pack?
Thus Venus; and Venus' son replied;
'No sister we of thine have spied
What name to call thee, beauteous maid?
That look, that voice the God betrayed,
Can it be Phoebus' sister bright
Or some fair Nymph, has crossed our sight?
Be gracious, whosoe'er thou art
And lift this burden from our heart.'

William Morris, the friend of Ruskin and admirer of things mediaeval, made a version of the *Aeneid* in the same metre as Thomas Phaer, but with greater success. We might expect even more archaisms than Morris actually uses. He very skilfully reproduces Virgil's word order, and he follows Virgil's text more closely than Conington, but the effect in the end is rather wooden. But judge for yourself:

Virgil in English

But as he reached the thicket's midst his mother stood before,
Who virgin face, and virgin arms, and virgin habit bore,
A Spartan maid; or like to her who tames the Thracian horse,
Harpalyce, and flies before the hurrying Hebrus' course.
For huntress-wise on shoulder she had hung the handy bow
And given all her hair abroad for any wind to blow,
And, naked-kneed, her kirtle long had gathered in a lap.
She spake the first: 'Ho youths,' she said, 'tell me by any hap
If of my sisters any one ye saw a wandering wide
With quiver girt, and done about with lynx's spotted hide,
Or following of the foaming boar with shouts and eager feet?'
So Venus; and so Venus' son began her words to meet:
'I have not seen, nor have I heard thy sisters nigh this place,
O maid:– and how to call thee then? for neither is thy face
Of mortals, nor thy voice of men: O very Goddess thou!
What! Phoebus' sister? or of nymphs whom shall I call thee now,
But whosoe'er thou be, be kind and lighten us our toil.'

In our own century it is no longer possible to reproduce the high rhetoric and abundance of adjectives that was part of the continuous tradition from Virgil up to the end of last century. It seems entirely proper to leave the last word with Virgil as mediated by the supple rhythms and style closer to a heightened natural speech of that fine poet, Cecil Day Lewis, who is far from the last translator of the 'divine poet' of the *Aeneid*. Notice how close he keeps to Virgil's words:

There, from the heart of the woodland, his mother came
  to meet him
Guised as a maiden in face and dress, with a girl's weapons –
A Spartan girl, as it might be, or Thracian Harpalyce,
Outpacer of horses, swift outrunner of running rivers.
In huntress wise she had handily slung her bow from her
  shoulder,

Virgil through the Ages

And her hair was free to blow in the wind, and she went
    bare-kneed
With the flowing folds of her dress kilted up and securely
    knotted.
She spoke first:–
      Hullo there, young men! If you have seen
One of my sisters roving hereabouts or in full cry
After a foaming boar – she carries a slung quiver
And wears a spotted lynx-skin – please tell me where she went.
Thus Venus spoke; and the son of Venus began to reply thus:–
No sight or sound have I had of any of your sisters,
O – but what shall I call you, maiden? for your face is
Unmortal, and your speech rings not of humankind.
Goddess surely you are. A nymph? The sister of Phoebus?
Give luck, whoever you be! Lighten, I pray, our ordeal!
Tell me in what clime, upon what shores of the world
We are cast up: for driven here by wind and wave,
We have no clue to the peoples or places of our wandering.
Tell this, and we will offer sacrifice at your altar.

(Aeneid 1. 314–36.

Selective Bibliography

VIRGIL LATIN TEXTS:
  R. A. B. Mynors (Oxford Classical Texts, 1969, second ed. 1972)
  H. R. Fairclough, with translation (Loeb, 2 vols, 1934–35)
  T. E. Page, with commentary (Macmillan, 3 vols, 1894–1900)
  R. D. Williams, with commentary (Macmillan, 3 vols, 1972–79)

VIRGIL TRANSLATIONS:
Verse: Dryden (1697)
    C. Day Lewis (1940–63)
    Rolfe Humphries (1951)
    A. Mandelbaum (1971)
Prose: E. V. Rieu, *Eclogues* (Penguin, 1949)
    W. F. Jackson Knight, *Aeneid* (Penguin, 1955)

LITERARY AND GENERAL STUDIES
  C. M. Bowra, *From Virgil to Milton* (London, 1945)
  W. A. Camps, *An Introduction to Virgil's Aeneid* (Oxford, 1969)
  J. Chalker, *The English Georgic* (London, 1969)
  Domenico Comparetti, *Virgil in the Middle Ages*, translated by E. F. M.
    Benecke (1895, reprinted London, 1966)
  D. R. Dudley, *Virgil*, 'Studies in Latin Literature and its Influence'
    (London, 1969)
  T. R. Glover, *Virgil* (London, 1904, 7th edition, 1942)
  Gilbert Highet, *The Classical Tradition* (Oxford, 1949)
  E. Nitchie, *Vergil and the English Poets* (New York, 1919)
  R. M. Ogilvie, *Latin and Greek. A History of the Influence of the Classics
    on English Life from 1600 to 1918* (London, 1964)
  Brooks Otis, *Virgil: a Study in Civilized Poetry* (Oxford, 1963)

Virgil through the Ages

M. C. J. Putnam, *The Poetry of the Aeneid* (Cambridge, Mass., and London, 1965)

M. C. J. Putnam, *Virgil's Pastoral Art* (Princeton, 1970)

Kenneth Quinn, *Virgil's Aeneid: a Critical Description* (London, 1968)

T. G. Rosenmeyer, *The Green Cabinet* (Berkeley, 1969) – on the *Eclogues*

L. P. Wilkinson, *The Georgics of Virgil* (Cambridge, 1969)

R. D. Williams, *Virgil*, 'Greece and Rome: New Surveys in the Classics No. 1 (Oxford, 1967)

R. D. Williams, *Aeneas and the Roman Hero* (London, 1973)

APPENDIX ONE

Latin Manuscripts of Virgil in the British Library

The descriptions, brief as they are, sometimes supplement the older catalogues. The information is laid out in the following order: (1) vellum or paper, (2) date, (3) where written, (4) number of folios, (5) dimensions in millimetres of the page and, in brackets, the ruled space, (6) number of columns and in brackets the width of the written column if different from (5), (7) number of lines in the column, (8) decoration, (9) scribe, (10) former owners, (11) bibliography. Not all these 'boxes' are filled. The dated manuscripts are described with facsimile reproductions in A. G. Watson, *Catalogue of Dated and Datable Manuscripts c.700–1600 in the Department of Manuscripts, British Library*, 1979, referred to as 'Watson'.

1. **Sloane MS 2510.** Georgics ff.2–52b preceded by the Introduction f.1.
   Paper. 15th century (1485? 1465?). Written in Italy. 52 folios.
   215 × 150 mm (148 × 100 mm). 1 column (80 mm wide) of 22 lines.
   Historiated initial f.2. Coloured initials with gold. Owned by 'Bernardinus' f.52b. Watson, vol. I, p. 168.

2. **Sloane MS 3738.** Aeneid 4:1–336 with notes ff.5–22b.
   Paper. 17th century. 187 × 150 mm (150 × 100 mm). 1 column of 9 lines.

3. **Additional MS 10300.** Epistulae Familiares of Johannes Armentarius, Andreas Denterius, Guillelmus de Bosco ff.1–14b etc, Historia Cymonis et Iphigenie ff.15–96, Virgil Eclogues 1–3 with commentary, and the introduction to Eclogue 4 ff.96b–119.
   Paper. 16th century. France. 122 folios. 210 × 157 mm (154 × 100 mm). 1 column of 8 lines. Illuminated initials ff.15, 40b, 59, 91. Owned by Richard Heber (1773–1833), lot 371 in his book sale.

4. **Additional MS 11355.** Eclogues ff.1–22b, Georgics ff.23–78b, Aeneid including 2:567–588 ff.79–328, Priapea ff.329–346b.
   Vellum. 15th century. Written in Italy. 346 folios. 165 × 105 mm

(112 × 65 mm). 1 column of 20 lines. Illuminated initials ff. 1, 23, 79, 329.

5. **Additional MS 11885.** Theocritus in Greek ff. 1–41b, Virgil's Eclogues 1:1–9:2 in Latin ff. 42–64b.

>Vellum. 15th century. Written in Italy. 64 folios. 190 × 125 mm (117 × 77 mm. 14 lines. ff. 1–41b; 120 × 88 mm. 15 lines. ff. 42–64b). 1 column. Illuminated border with animals. Owned by Samuel Butler Bishop of Lichfield.

6. **Additional MS 11952.** Eclogues ff. 1–15b, Georgics ff. 15b–51b, Aeneid omitting 2:567–588 ff. 52–224b.

>Vellum. 15th century. 224 folios. 246 × 156 mm (172 × 86 mm). 1 column of 29 lines. White vine scroll initials with gold and colours ff. 1, 52. Owned by the Nicolini family of Florence; Samuel Butler Bishop of Lichfield (his sale catalogue 416).

7. **Additional MS 11953.** Eclogue 1 (lacks verses 39–79), Aeneid 1, Eclogue 2, Aeneid 2, (omitting verses 567–588) . . . Aeneid 10, Moretum, Aeneid 11, Dirae, Aeneid 12.

>Paper (ff. 1, 9 vellum). 15th century. 281 folios. 180 × 130 mm (113 × 61 mm). 1 column (70 mm wide) of 19–20 lines. ff. 266–275 misbound. Space for initials. Written by several hands. Owned by Samuel Butler Bishop of Lichfield (his sale catalogue 417).

8. **Additional MS 11954.** Eclogues ff. 1–12b, Georgics ff. 13–44b, Aeneid beginning 'Ille ego' and including 2:567–588 ff. 45–185b, 'Aeneid 13' (i.e. the supplement by Mapheus Vegius) f. 185b.

>Paper. 15th century. Written in Italy. 195 folios. 423 × 280 mm (262 × 125 mm). 1 column of 36 lines. Borders ff. 1, 45; initials ff. 1, 13, 45. Owned by Samuel Butler Bishop of Lichfield (his sale catalogue 518).

9. **Additional MS 11955.** Eclogues ff. 1–16b, Georgics ff. 16b–57b, Aeneid omitting 2:567–588 ff. 58–244.

>Vellum. 15th century. 244 folios. 254 × 170 mm (170 × 94 mm). 1 column of 27 lines. Half border f. 58. Illuminated white vine scroll initials. Hand 1 ff. 1–57, Hand 2 ff. 58–244. Owned by Samuel Butler Bishop of Lichfield (his sale catalogue 413).

10. **Additional MS 11956.** Eclogues ff. 1–16, Georgics ff. 16b–56, Aeneid omitting 2:567–588 ff. 56b–237. Aeneid 1–6 carefully corrected.

>Vellum. 15th century. 237 folios. 245 × 155 mm (160 × 85 mm). 1 column (70 mm wide) of 29 lines. White vine scroll initials ff. 1, 56b. Gaps in text filled later. Owned by Samuel Butler Bishop of Lichfield (his sale catalogue 414).

Appendix One

11. **Additional MS 11957.** Eclogues ff.1–15b, Georgics ff.16–55, Aeneid omitting 2:567–588 ff.55–232.

    Paper. 15th century. Written in Italy. 233 folios. 215 × 142 mm (155 × 85 mm). 1 column of 28 lines. Red initials and titles. No prefaces. Owned by Samuel Butler Bishop of Lichfield (his sale catalogue 415).

12. **Additional MS 11958.** Eclogues ff.1–19, Aeneid omitting 2:567–588 ff.21–223.

    Paper. 15th century (1475–1485 watermarks). Written in Germany. 224 folios. 300 × 210 mm (226 × 113/220 × 107 mm). 1 column of 24–29 lines. Space for initials. 15th century German binding by Johannes Richenbach in Gyslingen for Bartholome Stolcz. Owned by Samuel Butler Bishop of Lichfield (his sale catalogue 519).

13. **Additional MS 11959.** Eclogues ff.1–24b, Georgics 1:1–2:13 ff.25–36b.

    Vellum. 15th century. Written in England. 36 folios. 287 × 200 mm (203 × 137 mm). 1 column. Units of four or five lines with commentary, the latter in a smaller hand. Flourished initials. Owned by Samuel Butler Bishop of Lichfield (his sale catalogue 521).

14. **Additional MS 11960.** Eclogues ff.2–18, Georgics ff.19–61b.

    Vellum. 15th century. Written in Italy. 62 folios. 267 × 177 mm (180 × 96 mm). 1 column of 27 lines. Illuminated white vine scroll initials ff.2, 19. Flourished initials ff.29, 39b, 50b. Wrapper (ff.1 + 62) is a legal record, 1427 or later. Owned by Samuel Butler Bishop of Lichfield (his sale catalogue 520).

15. **Additional MS 11961.** Georgics ff.2–44b, Eclogues ff.45–60.

    Paper. 15th century. 61 folios (f.61 vellum). 283 × 210 mm (178 × 128 mm). 1 column of 25 lines. Coloured initials. Owned by Jac. Menotti 1472; Samuel Butler Bishop of Lichfield (his sale catalogue 522).

16. **Additional MS 14815.** Eclogues ff.1–17, Georgics ff.17b–61b, Aeneid omitting 2:567–588 ff.62–262b.

    Vellum. 15th century. Written in Italy. 262 folios. 270 × 165 mm (168 × 98 mm). 1 column of 25 lines. Interlace illuminated border f.62 and initials. Red penwork borders. From the Cassano Library.

17. **Additional MS 16166.** Eclogues ff.10–20, Georgics ff.20b–48, Aeneid omitting 2:567–588 ff.54–184. Some folios added, some erased in favour of medical recipes mostly in English (ff.10–11b Eclogues 1:1–2:57, ff.47b–48 Georgics 4:473–503, 513–566, ff.54b–56b Aeneid 1:1–183).

    Vellum. 14th century. Written in England. 191 folios. 204 × 105 mm

Appendix One

(153 × 63 mm). 1 column of 40 lines. Owned by Thomas Warner f.2.

18. **Additional MS 16562.** Eclogues ff.3–16b with commentary and glosses. Georgics ff.17–53b, Appendix Vergiliana ff.54–69b, Priapea ff.70–81b, Epitaphia f.82.

   Paper (vellum outside leaves of gatherings). 15th century. Written in Italy. 82 folios. 292 × 211 mm (176 × 106 mm). 1 column of 30 lines. Space for initials. Date erased: 7, 10 July 14— (f.16b), 28 June (f.53b). Watson, vol. I p.165.

19. **Additional MS 17404.** Eclogues 7:63–10:77 ff.1–5, Georgics ff.6–41, Aeneid omitting 2:567–588 ff.42b–218, Statius Achilleid 1:1–2:133 ff.220–231b.

   Paper. 15th century. Written in Italy (iuxa for iussa f.88). 231 folios. 293 × 215 mm (200 × 100 mm). 1 column of 29 lines (21 lines ff.106–129 i.e. Aeneid 6). Gold initials ff.6, 43. Coloured initials. Scribe KPHBNFS i.e. Johanes.

20. **Additional MS 18151.** Aeneid omitting 2:567–588 ff.1–114b.

   Vellum. 14th century. 116 folios. 270 × 140 mm (203 × 70 mm). 1 column of 44 lines. Change of hand f.11.

21. **Additional MS 21910.** Aeneid 1:1–8:161 omitting 2:567–588 and lacking 6:451–816 ff.1–62b. Commentary f.1.

   Vellum. 11th century. Written in Germany. 62 folios. 314 × 195 mm (253 × 130 mm). 1 column (105 mm) of 42–47 lines. Ancient holes avoided by text (e.g. ff.38b–39). 4 fols. missing after f.50. 'liber de Rindorp maiori'. Bibl.: Steinmeyer *Die althochdeutschen Glossen* (1879–1922) iv, 494.

22. **Additional MS 22013.** Ovid Ars Amatoria ff.2–41b, Remedium Amoris ff.42–55b, Epistula Sapphus ff.56–59b, Pulex etc. ff.60–63b, Virgil Priapea ff.64–74b.

   Vellum. AD 1468–9. Written in Italy. 74 folios. 270 × 190 mm (185/200 × 100 mm). 1 column of 29 lines. Miniature f.1b, illuminated interlace border f.2. Scribe Jo. Pinz. Owned by 'Ni. Vulpis Vincentini', 'Georgii de ghisilieriis', arms of Ghislieri of Bologna. Bibl.: Watson 256 pl.719.

23. **Additional MS 23897.** Aeneid 3:1– end ff.1–142 (old foliation 26–167).

   Vellum. 14th century. Written in Italy. 142 folios. 276 × 190 mm (197 × 102 mm). 1 column (80 mm) of 33 lines. Palimpsest: land register 'Castri Franchi'. Scribe f.132 AN bartholomeo DREA.

24. **Additional MS 27304.** Aeneid ff.5–112b (omits 2:567–588; lacks 10:275–379, 486–890; 11:75–178; 12:76–176, 950–952. 12:479 repeated on ff.107b, 108).

Vellum. 13th century. ff.114 (lacks 1f. after f.94, 4 ff. after f.95, 1f. after f.96, 1f. after f.104, 1f. after f.112). 235 × 125 mm (186 × 63 mm). 1 column of 40–54 lines. Marginal notes. Gatherings of 8 numbered i–vii (–xiv), xi¹⁰ xiv¹⁰ lacks 1, 10. Flourished initials. Owned by Richard Shuttleworth, John Rudd, William Shuttleworth f.2 (17th century); Luke Yorker f.4b (18th century).

25. **Additional MS 30935.** Miscellaneous fragments: Aeneid 1:1–2:14 with glosses. 15th century. f.255.

26. **Additional MS 32319A.** Eclogues ff.4–13, Georgics ff.13–37b with 'Arguments', Aeneid omitting 2:567–588 ff.38–148b, Vita etc ff.148b–150b.
    Vellum (ff.2, 3 paper). 13th century. ff.150. 245 × 145 mm (191 × 74/87 mm). 1 column of 45 lines. Commentary and glosses. Coloured initials. Interlace initial f.38.

27. **Additional MS 39648.** Eclogues ff.1–15, Georgics ff.15b–53, Aeneid omitting 2:567–588 ff.53b–227.
    Vellum. 15th century. ff.ii + 227. 273 × 180 mm (171 × 92 mm). 1 column of 29 lines. Gatherings of 10 numbered A–Y. Inhabited vine scroll borders ff.1, 15b, 54. Coat of arms. Discreet corrections. Owned by Robert Curzon, 14th Baron Zouche.

28. **Additional MS 44943.** Fragments of paper manuscripts taken from the binding of *Missale Lingonense*, Paris 1491 (IB. 39833) incl. ff.1–4 Virgil: Primus habet Libicam etc f.1, Vir magnus bello nulli etc f.1b, Aeneid 1:43–52 f.2b, Aeneid 1:337–367 ff.3–3b, Aeneid 1:538–565 imperfect ff.4–4b.
    Paper. 15th century. 240 × 210 mm (150 × 110 mm). 1 column of 14 lines.

29. **Arundel MS 82.** Epitaphia f.1, Introduction and Vita ff.2–4b, Eclogues ff.5–18b, Georgics ff.19–55b, Aeneid with 'Arguments' omitting 2:567–588 ff.56–227, Aeneid 13 ff.227b–238, Cento of Proba ff.239–246, Epitome of Cicero ff.246b–248.
    Paper. 15th century. ff.248. 336 × 235 mm (231 × 120 mm). 1 column of 30 lines. Flourished initials.

30. **Arundel MS 133.** Cicero, Philippics ff.1–78 (3 hands), Isocrates *Lat.* ff.84–88 (hand 4), [Virgil] Ciris, Aetna, Elegia, Catalepton ff.89–120b, Arguments to Aeneid etc ff.102b–104b (hand 5), [Cicero] de proprietate sermonum ff.105–108b (hand 6).
    Paper (ff.89, 96 vellum). 15th century. ff.118. 290 × 115 mm (208 × 124 mm ff.1–78; 185 × 115 mm ff.79–88; 262 × 151 mm ff.89–104b; 204 × 121 mm ff.105–118). 1 column and (ff.89–104) 2 columns.

Appendix One

Owned by Bilibald Pirckheimer.

31. **Arundel MS 193.** Eclogues ff.1–21b, Georgics ff.22–77, Aeneid lacks 1:413–2:87, omits 2:567–588 ff.79–318b, Aeneid 13 ff.319–323.

    Paper. 1455, 1457. ff.323. 214 × 155 mm (150/160 × 80/100 mm. 1 column of 20 lines. ff.1–318; 155 × 55 mm. 2 columns of 38 lines. ff.319–323). 11 leaves missing (Aeneid 1:413–2:87) after f.89. ff.103–114 (Aeneid 2:88–565) precede f.90. Coloured initials. Scribe J. Pirckheimer (also scholia). Watson 450 pl.548.

32. **Burney MS 269.** Aeneid 1:82–12:887 lacks 1:576–656, omits 2:567–588 ff.1–120.

    Vellum. 13th century. ff.120. 227 × 125 mm (174 × 67 mm). 1 column of 35–41 lines. Gatherings of 12 numbered ii–xi. 1f. lost at beginning, 1f. at end, 1f. after f.6.

33. **Burney MS 270.** Aeneid, Ille ego, Ovidian verse prefaces, omitting 2:567–588 ff.1–185b.

    Vellum. 15th century. Italy. ff.185 (formerly pp.1–370). 263 × 163 mm (176 × 87 mm). 1 column of 27 lines. Gatherings of 10 (ii^{11} xix^6), numbered A–S. Full border interlace with coat of arms f.1. Illuminated initials. Stamped binding with some gold tooling.

34. **Burney MS 271.** Eclogues ff.1–16, Georgics ff.16b–56, Aeneid including 2:567–588 ff.57–236.

    Vellum. 15th century. Italy. ff.236 and paper fly-leaves. 193 × 120 mm (126 × 70 mm). 1 column of 28 lines. L-border f.1, I-border f.57. White vine scroll initials.

35. **Burney MS 272.** Eclogues ff.4–17, Georgics ff.18–52b, Aeneid 1:1–12:300 omitting 2:567–588 ff.54–206, Moretum etc ff.207–210, Eclogues 1:1–6:23 ff.211–218, Commentary on Georgics 4 ff.219–223. Verse prefaces.

    Paper (f.2 vellum). 15th century. ff.223. 294 × 210 mm (192 × 94 mm). 1 column of 32 lines. Historiated initials cf. early woodcuts.

36. **Burney MS 273.** Aeneid omitting 2:567–588 ff.1–115.

    Vellum. 13th century. ff.116. 238 × 115 mm (201 × 85 mm). 1 column of 43 lines. Flourished initials.

37. **Burney MS 274.** Eclogues ff.1–17b, Georgics ff.18–57b, Aeneid ff.58–236b (2:567–588 in margin f.83, lacks 4:1–41, 266–321).

    Vellum. 15th century. ff.236. 181 × 129 mm (120 × 60 mm). 1 column of 28 lines. Lacks one folio after f.99, one folio after f. 103. Initials in gold and colours ff.1, 18, 59 (border and arms). Owners: Antonius Alamannus, Hermannus Alamanus, Angelus Alamanus, 'adnotationes Pauli Manuti'. Initial letters of names corrected to capitals.

38. **Burney MS 276.** Miscellaneous fragments: Aeneid 1:133–202 f.43, 1:467–502 f.44. 15th century. Italy. 302 × 200 mm (160 × 108 mm). 1 column (85 mm) of 35 lines.

39. **Burney MS 277.** Miscellaneous fragments: Aeneid 1:61–120 f.73. 15th century. 321 × 227 mm (218 × 105 mm). 1 column of 30 lines.

40. **Harley MS 2457.**Aeneid 5:155–7:335 ff.1–31, 7:786–8:79 ff.33–34, 10:467–908 ff.35–41, 11:53–886 ff.42–54, 12:18–401 ff.55–60, 12:467–915 ff.61–67b, Eclogues 1:16–78 ff.68–68b, 3:47–10:77 ff.69–78b, Georgics 1:117–3:198 ff.79–96b, 4:333–525 ff.97–99b.

    Vellum. 15th century. ff.99. 280 × 195 mm (180 × 112 mm). 1 column of 32 lines. Gatherings of 10 (f.32 a stub, 6ff. lost after f.32, 3off. lost after f.34, 1f. lost after f.41, 1f. lost after f.54, 1f. after f.60, 2ff. after f.68, 2ff. after f.78, 11ff. after f.96). White vine scroll initial f.12. Others cut out ff.26b, 33b, 41b. Damaged by water. Owned by Nathaniel Noel.

41. **Harley MS 2472.** Aeneid ff.1–141, omitting 2:567–588, added in margin.

    Vellum. 15th century. Italy. ff.141. 286 × 195 mm (190 × 115 mm). 1 column (75 mm) of 36 lines. Gatherings i–xiv¹⁰. Border f.1. Illuminated initials. Gold-tooled Harley binding. Owners: 'Brunon' f.141b (Leonardi Bruno?); Nathaniel Noel.

42. **Harley MS 2473.** Genealogy of the gods ff.1–4, Names of rivers f.4, Commentary on Aeneid f.5, Aeneid with verse preface, including 2:567–588 ff.5b–168.

    Paper. 15th century. Italy (watermark Briquet 6588, 6591, 6592, 6595). ff.1*, 169. 290 × 200 mm (173 × 92 mm). 1 column of 31 lines. Signatures a1 etc. Owners: Daniel Browne; John Chamberlayne.

43. **Harley MS 2501.** Aeneid omitting 2:567–588 ff.1–160.

    Paper. 1466. Italy. ff.162. 308 × 210 mm (206 × 92 mm). 1 column of 30–31 lines. Initial A f.1. Interlinear glosses throughout, marginal commentary ff.1–3b, 62b–75 (Aeneid 6). Scribe Gabriel Gnuardus de Asula f.160. Owner: Nathaniel Noel. Watson 658 pl.689.

44. **Harley MS 2502.** Eclogues ff.1–13 (f.2 Eclogues 6:44–7:24 should come after f.8), Georgics ff.13–46, Aeneid 1:1–7:233 omitting 2:567–588 ff.47–116, fragment of Pindar, epitome Iliados *Lat.* ff.116–123b, Aeneid 7:234–699 ff.123b–129, 129b–130b, 129–129b, Aeneid 6:219–684 ff.130b–137b. These dislocations suggest that the exemplar had 29 lines per page.

    Paper. 1465, 1470. ff.137, old foliation i–cxliii. 298 × 195 mm (224 × 132 mm). 1 column of 33 lines. Spaces for initials. Scribe Antonius de Saluanezio. Owned by John Gibson. Watson 659 pl.680.

45. **Harley MS 2503.** Eclogues ff.1–8b, Georgics with verse preface ff.9b–30, Aeneid with verse preface, omitting 2:567–588 ff.31–115. Commentary and glosses.

    Paper. 15th century. ff.115. 300 × 200 mm (265 × 82 mm). 1 column of 57 lines. ff.61, 72 misbound. Owners: 'Lecomte' f.(–1); 'Petri Dupuy' f.1; Andrew Hay.

46. **Harley MS 2533.** Eclogues ff.1–14b, Georgics ff.14b–48b.

    Vellum. 13th century. South France? ff.48. 256 × 160 mm (200 × 92 mm). 1 column of 31 lines. (f.48b 2 columns of 69, 72 lines). Gatherings i–vi⁸. Drawing of city f.13, animal interlace initial f.14b, coloured diagram of world f.18b. Owned by Jesuit College of Agen.

47. **Harley MS 2534.** Eclogues ff.2–9b, Georgics ff.10–30b, notes ff.31–31b, Aeneid omitting 2:567–588 ff.32–126, Copa etc ff.126b–129b. Commentary and glosses.

    Vellum. 13th century. ff.130. 242 × 126 mm (187 × 70 mm). 1 column of 53 lines. Gatherings i⁸ (ff.2–9) ii–iii⁸ iv⁶ (end Georgics) v–x⁸ xi¹⁰ xii–xv⁸ xvi⁹. Owned by Jesuit College of Agen f.1.

48. **Harley MS 2553.** Aeneid omitting 2:567–588 ff.1–249.

    Paper. 1442. ff.249. 212 × 145 mm (85/105 × 60/65 mm). 1 column of 20 lines. Coloured initials. f.73 should come after f.68, f.76 after f.67. Scribe Johannes f.248. Watson 668 pl.452.

49. **Harley MS 2555.** Patristic fragment from binding f.1★, Juvenal ff.1–78, Persius ff.79–92b, Ovid Ep. Sapph. ff.92b–95b, Virgil Eclogues 1:1–6:23 ff.96–104b, 10:3–77 ff.105–106, Georgics ff.106b–150b.

    Paper. 15th century. ff.1★, 152. 215 × 140 mm (140 × 95 mm). 1 column of 25 lines. Owned by Jesuit College of Agen.

50. **Harley MS 2578.** Fragment from binding ff.1, 301, Table of contents f.2b, Hesiod *Lat.* ff.4–22b, Calpurnius ff.25–41b, Nemesianus ff.42–49, Petrarch Bucolica 1–12 ff.57–94, Theocritus *Lat.* ff.95–123, Virgil Eclogues, Priapea ff.127–168b, Ausonius ff.169–260b (including Cento Nuptialis of Virgilian lines), Proba Virgilian Cento ff.261–277, P. Gregorius Tifernes ff.277b–300.

    Paper. circa 1499? Italy. ff.301. 204 × 140 mm (131 × 80 mm). 1 column of 22–25 lines. Owned by John Gibson. Bibl.: Giarratano, *Calpurnii et Nemesiani Bucolica*, 1910, p.xxiv.

51. **Harley MS 2644.** Liber fabularum ff.1–22, Virgil Eclogues ff.22b–35b, Georgics 1:1–4:136 with verse preface ff.35–67.

    Vellum. 12th/13th century. Germany. ff.67. 200 × 125 mm (160 × 110 mm ff.1–16; 170 × 90 mm ff.17–67). 1 column of 28–37 lines. Harley gold-tooled binding. Owned by Nathaniel Noel.

Appendix One

52. **Harley MS 2668.** Eclogues ff.1–4, Georgics 1:1–4:529 ff.4–13, Aneid 1:1–4:678 omitting 2:567–588, lacking 3:531–590, omitting 4:528 ff.13–24b.

> Vellum. 12th century. ff.24. 294 × 180 mm (251 × 139 mm). 2 columns of 60–63 lines. Gatherings of 8, numbered 'primus', 'ii', 'iii'. Harley gold-tooled binding. Owned by St Nicolas of Cues; Nathaniel Noel.

53. **Harley MS 2695.** Eclogues ff.1–24, Aeneid 6 ff.25–46b, Moretum ff.47–49b, Ovid ep Sapph ff.50–55b, Venantius Fortunatus ff.55b–58, Lactantius Phoenix ff.58–62, Batrachomyomachia *Lat.* ff.62–70, grammatica ff.70–75b (explicit: hoc scripsi totum per Christum da mihi potum), Ovid Fasti 2:679–852 ff.76–80b, arms ff.81–82, sententiae morales and notes ff.84–92.

> Paper. 15th century. Italy. ff.92. 141 × 100 mm (85 × 65 mm). 1 column of 17–18 lines. Owned by 'Guelfus' f.1★; Paul Vaillant. Harley gold-tooled binding.

54. **Harley MS 2701.** Eclogues ff.2–19b, Georgics ff.19b–66, Aeneid omitting 2:567–588 ff.67–276b, Appendix ff.277–310.

> Vellum. 1487. Rome. ff.310. 164 × 100 mm (125 × 70 mm). 1 column of 24 lines. Gatherings of 10. White vine scroll initials with gold and colours. Scribe Johannes olim Benedicti de Florentia. Owners: 'G. Baruffaldi' f.1; 'Andrea Haii Venetia 1722' (Andrew Hay) f.1b; 'Hic codex olim fuit Aldi Manuti' acc. to Wanley. Watson 693 pl.490.

55. **Harley MS 2706.** Epitaphia f.1, Eclogues 1:1–10:43 ff.3–22b, Aeneid omitting 2:567–588 ff.23–269b, Verses on Aeneid ff.269b–271.

> Vellum. 15th century. ff.271. 163 × 100 mm (120 × 50 mm). 1 column of 20 lines. Gatherings of 10. Owned by Nathaniel Noel. Harley gold-tooled binding.

56. **Harley MS 2726.** Aeneid with verse preface f.1b, Ille ego, omitting 2:567–588 ff.2–194b.

> Vellum. 1463. Italy. ff.194. 238 × 160 mm (163 × 91 mm). 1 column of 26 lines. Gatherings of 10. Illuminated A, border, arms f.2. Initials. Scribe Franciscus de Camuciis f.194b. Owners: Aegidius de Busleyden; Colleg. Buslidianum Lovanii; Daniel Browne; John Chamberlayne. Watson 697 pl.650.

57. **Harley MS 2744.** Eclogues ff.1–11, Georgics ff.11–39, Aeneid omitting 2:567–588 ff.39–180b, Proba Cento ff.181–191b, Statius Achilleid 1:1–2:438 ff.193–208b.

> Vellum. early 15th century. Italy. ff.208. 267 × 180 mm (172 × 97 mm). 1 column of 35 lines (ff.1–24 late 15th century. 41

lines). Gatherings of 8. Space for initials, some flourished initials. Owners: 'Lelii Capilupi codex'; Nathaniel Noel. Harley gold-tooled binding.

58. **Harley MS 2754.** Eclogues ff.1–12, Georgics ff.12–41, Aeneid omitting 2:567–588 ff.42–174.

   Vellum. 15th century. ff.174. 257 × 170 mm (193 × 90 mm). 1 column of 38 lines. Gatherings of 10. Flourished initials and red and blue initials. Owners: Browne; Chamberlayne. Harley gold-tooled binding.

59. **Harley MS 2755.** Aeneid omitting 2:567–588 ff.1–180, Eclogues ff.181–195b, Georgics 1:1–4:558 ff.196–234.

   Vellum. 15th century. ff.234. 260 × 170 mm (163 × 102 mm). 1 column of 28 lines. Gatherings of 12. Border f.1 with blank shield for arms. Initials ff.1, 15, 29, 42 etc. Scribe Augustinus de Tervisio, Parma. Text carefully corrected by a hand of circa 1550–1600.

60. **Harley MS 2761.** Eclogues ff.1–35, Georgics ff.35–55b, Aeneid including Ille ego, omitting 2:567–588 ff.55b–239b.

   Vellum. 15th century (Florence 1450–1470?). ff.1*, 1–239. 250 × 150 mm (159 × 80 mm). 1 column of 28 lines. Gatherings of 10. Full border f.1, part border f.55b, initials. Owned by Gibson. Harley gold-tooled binding.

61. **Harley MS 2770.** Aeneid with verse preface f.1b, omitting 2:567–588 ff.2–54.

   Vellum. 13th century. ff.54. 281 × 175 mm (225 × 132 mm). 2 columns of 48 lines. Gatherings of 8, numbered i, ii, and 2–7. Marginalia. 'Flor. P. Pothenii'. Owners: Graevius; G. G. Zamboni.

62. **Harley MS 2772.** Fragments bound together:

   I. Aeneid 7:394–8:147, 8:220–291, 8:364–652, 10:450–522, 11:900–12:43, 11:684–755. ff.1–15b.

      Vellum. 10th century. 1 column of 36–38 lines. Ruled for commentary. $i^8 ii^7$.

   II. Juvenal 11:154–14:160. ff.16–25b. 10th century (225 × 105 mm). 1 column of 30 lines. i^{10}.

   III. Juvenal 13:234–14:110 ff.26–27b. 10th century (220 × 118 mm). 1 column of 32 lines.

   IV. Sedulius Carmen Paschale 1.198–4.12 ff.28–43b. (198 × 119 mm). 1 column of 27 lines. $i^8 ii^8$.

   V. Macrobius Commentary on Somnium Scipionis 1.2.2–2.15.8 ff.44–74b. (208 × 150 mm). 1 column of 38 lines. $i^6 ii^9 iii^8 iv^8$.

   VI. Fragm. of ancient commentary on Juvenal. 17th century. ff.75–82.

VII. Paraphrase of Juvenal. 17th century. ff.83–90. Graevius; Zamboni.

63. **Harley MS 2777.** Aeneid omitting 2:567–588 ff.1–98b, epitaph etc ff.98b–99b.

Vellum. 13th century. ff.99. 281 × 115 mm (222 × 70 mm). 1 column of 51 lines. Gatherings of 8, ff.32–39, 40–47 pricked on 1 recto when folded. Brown morocco binding with central lozenge.

64. **Harley MS 3072.** Miscellaneous fragments:

I. Eclogues 2:32–3:74 ff.1–2. 10th century. 249 × 180 mm (187 × 97 mm). 1 col of 29 lines. Red and silver rubrics oxidized.

II. Sedulius, Arator, etc. 10th–11th century. ff.3–87. (185–210 × 100–110 mm). 1 column of 30 lines.

III. Servius Commentary on Georgics 1:56–63, 70–93, 186–218. ff.94, 103. 9th century. 250 × 180 mm (at least 250 × at least 155 mm). 1 column of 36+ lines. Text in Caroline minuscules, annotated words in red uncials. Matthew de Varenne 1723.

65. **Harley MS 3440.** Introduction and Eclogues ff.1b–15b, Introduction and Georgics ff.16b–52b, [Seneca] de Remediis fortuitorum ff.52b–54b.

Vellum. 1409. Italy. ff.54. 237 × 160 mm (165 × 88 mm). 1 column of 31 lines. (ff.53–54: 195 × 134 mm. 38 lines). i–ii⁸ iii⁹ iv–vi⁸ vii⁴. Scribe Sozomeno of Pistoia. Owners: Gibson. Bibl.: A. C. de la Mare, *Das Verhältnis der Humanisten zur Buch*, 1977, p.103. Watson 752 pl.322.

66. **Harley MS 3518.** Aeneid with verse preface, Ille ego, including 2:567–588 ff.1–201b, extract from Servius on Aeneid 6 f.202.

Paper. 1454. Palermo. ff.203. 193 × 143 mm (150 × 70 mm). 1 column of 25 lines. Colophon f.201b. Owners: 'Dons. Justus' f.1, Andreas f.24b, Franc. Lenzi f.203b, 'Stefani' f.203b; Gibson. Harley goldtooled binding. Watson 761 pl.544.

67. **Harley MS 3754.** Eclogues ff.1–4b (lacks Eclogues 6:83–8:40, the outer columns of ff.3, 3b), Georgics ff.4b–14b, Aeneid with verse preface, omitting 2:567–588 ff.15–61, Lucan ff.61b–101, Statius Thebaid 1:1–6:482 ff.101–120b, Horace ff.121–155b, Persius ff.156–159, Juvenal ff.159–159b, Ovid Metamorphoses 1 with gaps ff.160–173.

Vellum. 15th century. Italy. ff.173. 410 × 290 mm (300 × 195 mm). 2 columns of 55 lines. Gatherings of 10. Some initials, spaces for others. Owned by Jesuit College of Agen.

68. **Harley MS 3944.** Service book f.1*, Aeneid omitting 2:567–588 ff.1–126, list of kings of Rome f.126, Eclogues with verse preface ff.126b–137, Georgics ff.137b–164b.

Vellum. 15th century (f.1* x). ff.1*, 1–164. 270 × 145 mm

(206 × 69 mm). 1 column of 39 lines. Gatherings of 8. Owned by Andrew Hay.

69. **Harley MS 3955.** Italian legal treatise ff.1, 133, Notes in the hand of Sozomeno of Pistoia ff.3–9b, Aeneid with verse preface, Ille ego ff.10–130, Aeneid 2:567–588 f.130b, Notes from Servius on Aeneid 6 f.131.

Paper. 1385. Italy. ff.133. 290 × 210 mm (197 × 104 mm). 1 column of 41 lines. Gatherings (ff.10–130 formerly 1–121) i¹² ii¹⁰ iii–x¹² xi⁵. Scribe (?) Stefanus Silius olim Simonis Ser Michaelis. Owners: Stefani 418 (i.e. 1418), Giovanni, Bernardo Gherardo, Bandinellus. Watson 797 pl.275.

70. **Harley MS 3963.** Eclogues ff.1–16b, Georgics ff.16b–57b, Aeneid including (marked +) 2:567–588 ff.57b–245, Appendix ff.245–263, Epitaphs etc ff.263–268.

Vellum. 15th century. ff.268. 350 × 210 mm (215 × 123 mm). 1 column of 27 lines.

71. **Harley MS 4097.** Aeneid with verse preface, omitting 2:567–588 ff.2–152b, Marginal commentary to f.50 (5:144), Summa preceptorum ff.153, 153b.

Vellum and paper (vellum inner and outer sheets of each gathering). 15th century. ff.153. 293 × 220 mm (196 × 91 mm). 1 column of 32–34 lines. i² ii–xiv¹² xv⁸. Mattheus de Luca notarius 1410 f.153.

72. **Harley MS 4098.** Aeneid omitting 2:567–588 ff.1–155b.

Paper. 15th century (circa 1440 f.1*b). Italy. ff.1*, 1–155. 286 × 200 mm (188 × 107 mm). 1 column of 32 lines. Historiated initial f.1. Flourished initials. Owners: Bartholomeus de Mazaborinis, Federicus de Lando, Manfredo de Lando.

73. **Harley MS 4856.** Eclogues pp.1–30, Georgics with verse preface pp.31–109, Aeneid with verse preface, omitting 2:567–588 pp.110–466, Tetrasticha Ovidii pp.466–469.

Vellum. 15th century. Italy. pp.469. 250 × 150 mm (180 × 91 mm). 1 column of 28 lines. Gatherings of 12 a–s. pp.171–190 (12:123–626) and pp.435–454 (3:151–710) transposed. Illuminated initials.

74. **Harley MS 5198.** Persius ff.1–15, Claudian de raptu Proserpinae ff.15–39, [Ovid] de vocibus ff.39–40b, Epigrams of Virgil, Gallus etc ff.40b–42, Virgil Moretum with variant readings ff.42b–44b, Death of Astyanax translated by Mapheus Vegius ff.44b–51, Ovid ep Sapph ff.51b–55b, Batrachomyomachia latine ff.55b–62, Donatus de barbarismo ff.62b–70b, De arte dicendi ff.71–105. No commentary.

Paper. 15th century. ff.105. 192 × 142 mm (140 × 83 mm). 1 column of 25 lines. i⁴ ii–iv¹⁰ v–vi¹² vii¹⁰ viii–x¹² xi⁶. Owner: 'Stephani de bertolinis et amicorum eius' f.105b.

75. **Harley MS 5209.** Tibullus ff.1–43, Ovid ep Sapph ff.43b–48, Lactantius Phoenix ff.48b–52, Virgil Moretum ff.52–54b, Ovid Pont 1.1–2.7.18 ff.55–78.

Vellum. 15th century. Italy(?). ff.78. 199 × 135 mm (135 × 81 mm). 1 column of 23 lines. (ff.1–52); 27 lines. (ff.52b–78). i–v⁸ vi¹⁰ vii¹² viii–ix⁸. Red titles faded. Darkened by reagent. Owned by Jesuit College of Agen.

76. **Harley MS 5261.** Eclogues ff.1–18, Georgics ff.18b–63, Aeneid with verse preface, omitting 2:567–588 ff.63b–266b (f.91b 'hic erant versus helene'), Epitaphia etc ff.267–268.

Vellum. 15th century (humanist). ff.268. 234 × 165 mm (143 × 100 mm). 1 column of 25 lines. Gatherings of 10, numbered beg. A–V etc. Full border with arms of Maffei family of Volterra. White vine scroll initials, interlace initials, historiated initials. Scribe Johannes de Parma (cypher ff.63, 266b). Collated with 'Cod. Romanus' ff.7b, 22b, 23, 53, 133 (et Longobardico).

77. **Harley MS 5268.** Aeneid with verse preface including 2:567–588 ff.1–203.

Vellum. late 15th century. Italy. ff.203 (pp.1–416). 240 × 155 mm (170 × 91 mm). 1 column of 25 lines. i–xx¹⁰. White vine scroll initials with gold and colours. Erased coat of arms. Reagent e.g. f.59b. Some leaves palimpsest (ff.54, 71).

78. **Kings MS 24.** Eclogues ff.1–16b, Georgics ff.17–58, Aeneid with verse preface, omitting 2:567–588 ff.59–244b.

Vellum. 15th century. Italy. ff.245 (f.245 paper). 284 × 175 mm (194 × 100 mm). 1 column of 28 lines. i–v¹⁰ vi⁸ vii–xxiii¹⁰ xxiv⁶, A–AA. Full border with coat of arms probably Ludovico Agneli, Bp. of Cosenza 1497–1499 f.1, other full borders and lesser illum. Running titles in blue, numerals in gold. Scribe Bartolomeo Sanvito. Rare marginalia, some variant readings. Owners: 'Sagredo'. Joseph Smith.

79. **Kings MS 25.** Eclogues omitting 2:44–47 ff.1–15, Georgics omitting 3:56 ff.15b–53b, Nocte pluit etc f.54b, Aeneid with verse preface, Ille ego, omitting 2:567–588, 7:587, 8:272, 569, 9:29, 10:278–279, 285, 11:205 ff.55–228b.

Vellum. 15th century. ff.i, 1–228. 182 × 120 mm (123 × 65 mm). 1 column of 29 lines. Gatherings of 10 (iv⁴ last⁶). Small illuminated initials ff.1, 55b, decorated initials Georgics, Aeneid, flourished initials Eclogues 2–10. 18th century vellum binding.

80. **Royal MS 8 F.xiv.** Theological tracts by Hugo de S. Victore and

others, 13th and 14th centuries. ff.204. 280 × 190 mm. Bury St Edmunds Abbey, 'per fratrem Henricum de Kirkstede'. Fly-leaves from binding ff.1–6. ff.1–2 philosophical fragments, 13th century. ff.3–4 Aeneid 8:302–425 with interlinear and marginal scholia.

> Vellum. 11th century. 250 × 190 mm (215 × 110 mm). 1 column of 31 lines. Offsets on ff.2b, 5. Inner bifolium of a gathering.

81. **Royal MS 15 B.iv.** Music ff.1–3, 122, 123, Aeneid including 2:567–588 ff.4–121, Notes on Virgil (14th century) f.122b.

> Vellum. 13th century. ff.123. 243 × 120 mm (193 × 63 mm). 1 column of 40 lines. Gatherings of 8 (xv⁶). Initials in colours, but few inserted. Owned by St Augustine's Abbey, Canterbury.

82. **Royal MS 15 B.xxi.** Eclogues ff.2–17, Georgics ff.17–57, Aeneid with verse preface, Ille ego, omitting 2:567–588 ff.57–237.

> Vellum. 15th century. ff.238. 260 × 180 mm (174 × 97 mm). 1 column of 28 lines. i¹⁰ etc numbered A–Z. beg. and end. White vine scroll initials with gold, some also with blue and green. Owners: Johannes de Flandria f.2; 'Ex Libris Claudii Expillii 1592' [President of Parlement de Grenoble d.1636] ff.1, 237.

83. **Lansdowne MS 834.** Facsimile of Vatican Vergil (Vat. lat. 3225: 'F') made by Pietro Santi Bartoli, AD 1677. All 50 pictures are reproduced in colour, but the text is reproduced only up to Aeneid 4.310: Georgics 3:1–21, 146–214, 285–348, Georgics 4:97–124, 153–174, 471–497, 522–548, Aeneid 1:185–268, 419–521, 586–611, 654–680, Aeneid 2:170–198, 254–309, 437–468, 673–699, Aeneid 3:1–54, 79–216, 300–341, 600–689, Aeneid 4:1–92, 234–257, 287–310.

Latin Manuscripts of Virgil in the British Library: Commentaries and Anthologies

1. **Sloane MS 3371.** ff.20–20b.
   Notes on Aeneid 6:806–817. 17th century. 198 × 155 mm.
2. **Additional MS 9784.** Servius Commentary on Eclogues ff.1–46b, Commentary on Georgics ff.47–117.
   Paper. 1459. ff.117. Italy. 290 × 205 mm (170 × 105 mm ff.1–46; 198 × 105 mm ff.47–117). 1 column of 28 lines. (ff.1–46); 35 lines (ff.47–117). Watson 13 pl.585.
3. **Additional MS 10095.** Benvenuto de Ymola on Eclogues, Georgics ff.3–106, Pacis on Geoffrey of Vinsauf's Poetica Novella ff.108–156, Commentary on Theobald of Piacenza ff.158b–163b, Bonaconsa on Horace ff.164–176b, Horace Ars Poetica with notes ff.177–182b, Statius Achilleid with notes ff.183–196, Commentary on Statius Achilleid ff.197–222b.
   Paper. 15th century (ff.108–156 1427). ff.222. 295 × 210 mm (205 × 157 mm). 2 columns of 37–41 lines. Watson 21 pl.390.
4. **Additional MS 15341.** Commentary on Eclogues 1–10.
   Paper. 1497 (Milan?). ff.108. 195 × 135 mm (133 × 88 mm). 1 column of 24 lines. Scribe Andreas de Sormano f.108b. Watson 129 pl.885.
5. **Additional MS 16380.** Commentary 'Glosule Eneidos' on Aeneid, Georgics ff.1–91, Commentary on Juvenal ff.92–110, Commentary on Statius ff.144–179, etc.
   Vellum. 15th century. ff.307. 231 × 160 mm (180 × 125 mm). 2 columns of 52 lines.
6. **Additional MS 17414.** Servius on Georgics 1 ff.1–65b, Henricus Florentinus ff.67–85, Grammatica ff.86–92, Petrus Diaconus de historia Romae ff.95–96b.
   Paper. 15th century. ff.109. 216 × 143 mm (134 × 75 mm ff.1–65; rest various).

7. **Additional MS 18459.** Poetical anthology based on the Speculum Historiale of Vincent of Beauvais. 'De Virgilio, de dictis eius, et floribus Virgilii' ff.3b–4 including Eclogues 2:61, 65, 3:60, 92–93, 4:5–7, 5:36–37, 8:63, 71, 75, 10:19, 69 and extracts from Georgics and Aeneid.
   Vellum. 14th century. ff.30. 147 × 104 mm (119 × 85 mm). 2 columns of 31 lines.

8. **Additional MS 33220.** Commentary on Eclogues, Georgics, Aeneid. Lacks parts of Eclogues 1, 2, 4, 6, all of 5, Aeneid 12:12–end.
   Vellum. 13th century. Italy. ff.84.

9. **Additional MS 33795.**Servius, Commentary on Virgil Eclogues, Georgics. 1464. Scribe Nicolaus de Haga. ff.2–82; Commentary on Juvenal. 1473. Scribe Joh. Alues., Louvain. ff.88–193.

10. **Additional MS 34880.** E. Gibbon, Miscellaneous Works. Two tracts on Virgil ff.90, 93. 1757.

11. **Arundel MS 268.**Two volumes of astronomical tracts:
    I.   ff.1–74b. Vellum. 218 × 155 mm (180 × 100 mm). 2 columns of 46 lines. Spaces for diagrams.
    II. ff.75–103. Paper. 15th century. 230 × 160 mm (187 × 115 mm). 2 columns of 45 lines and (ff.92b–103) 1 column.
         Cento of Virgilian lines on astronomy ff.92b–95b.

12. **Burney MS 178.** Horace ff.1–99, Epitaphia on Virgil f.102.
    Vellum. 13th century (ff.1b, 2b 15th century). ff.102. 196 × 105 mm (156 × 65 mm). 1 column of 40 lines. Gatherings of 8 numbered i etc.

13. **Harley MS 2745.** [Ovid] de Vetula etc ff.1–48b, flor. Ovid ff.49–76b, flor. Tibullus etc ff.76b–84, flor. Homer ff.84–84b, flor. Virgil Eclogues, Georgics ff.84b–87b, flor. Statius, Prudentius, Horace, Boethius, Thobias, Aesop ff.87b–153, [Ovid] de Vetula ff.153–160.
    Vellum. 14th century. ff.160. 258 × 170 mm (180 × 80 mm). 1 column of 32 lines. Gatherings of 8. Rubricated.

14. **Royal MS 10 A.x.**
    I.   2 canon law tracts ff.1–146. 14th century. 240 × 167 mm (174 × 113 mm). 2 columns of 54 lines. Notes by John Theyer.
    II. Theological tracts ff.147–186b, Writ of execution f.187, Historia Troiana ff.188–192b, Servius Vita etc ff.192b–193b.
         Vellum. 13th century. 240 × 167 mm (199 × 146 mm). 2 columns of 45 lines. Owners: Henry Savile of Banke; Theyer sale catalogue 142.

15. **Royal MS 15 B.xix.**
    I.   Sedulius, Carmen pascale etc. Vellum. 10th century. ff.1–35. 255 × 160 mm (170 × 105 mm). 1 column of 28 lines. Gatherings of 8.

Appendix Two

II. Persius, Bede etc, including [Virgil] de sua nutrice, de imagine et somno f.99b, 'Versus Virgilii de se et Homero' f.102b. Vellum. 9th and 10th centuries. ff.36–199. 250 × 160 mm (185 × 110 mm). 1 column of 25 lines. Gatherings of 8.

III. Poems of Symposius and St Boniface. Vellum. 11th century. ff.200–205. 255 × 170 mm. (225 × 120 mm). 1 column (85, 70 mm) of 42 lines.

APPENDIX THREE

Manuscript Translations of Virgil in the British Library

1. **Sloane MS 836.**Aeneid translated by Sir E. Sherburne. 17th century. ff.49–50b.
2. **Sloane MS 900.** The Fingallian Travesty, or the sixth book of Virgills Aenaeids a la mode de Fingaule, 17th century.
3. **Sloane MS 3208,** ff.96–128b Translated into English by the Earl of Lauderdale: Georgics 1 ff.96–111, Georgics 2 ff.113–119b, 126b–128, Georgics 3:1–399 ff.120–125.
4. **Additional MS 18178.** Aeneid translated into Genoese by G. B. Torello, 17th century.
5. **Additional MS 27346.** Translations from the Aeneid in verse by Lord Lauderdale, 1689–1691.
6. **Additional MS 27347.** Translations of Mapheus Vegius' addition to the Aeneid by R. Waller, 1674. With autograph drawings imitating the engravings in Ogilby's Virgil, 1654.
    Paper. ff.49. 360 × 230 mm.
7. **Additional MS 28644.** Translation from the Aeneid in English verse by C. Montagu. f.96. 17th century.
8. **Additional MS 36529.** Translation of Aeneid 1–3 by T. Phaer. ff.10–20 (Aeneid 1), 21–29b (Aeneid 2), 36–43 (Aeneid 3). 1555–1557.
9. **Additional MS 38488A.** Notes on Georgics 1, 2 ff.66–137, Translations of Georgics 3, 4 ff.138–194. Circa 1771.
10. **Additional MS 60283.** English translation of Aeneid 4 in 6-line rhymed stanzas attributed to Sir John Haryngton.
11. **Burney MS 276.** Translation into Greek of Eclogue 1:50–77, 1–49. ff.41–52b. 16th century.
12. **Hargrave MS 205.** Translation into English of Aeneid 4 by Henry Howard, Earl of Surrey, 16th century.
13. **Royal MS 16 C.viii.** Greek translation of Aeneid 1 by Joh. Harpsfeld of

Appendix Three

Oxford, circa 1530–1550.

Paper. ff.42. 187 × 130 mm (126 × 115 mm). 1 column of 9 lines.
Owners: 'Thomas Cantuaren.' f.1, Lumley f.2b.

14. **Egerton MS 167.** Translations into Irish by L. Smith of Ovid, Horace,
Theocritus, and Virgil Eclogue 2 (ff.2–3), Eclogue 3 (ff.6b–7b), Eclogue
5 (ff.13—14), Eclogue 8 (ff.16–17b), Eclogue 6 (ff.26–27), Eclogue 7
(ff.27b–28b), Eclogue 10 (ff.28b–30), Eclogue 9 (ff.55b–56b). 1709–
1710.